Late Invocation for Magic

OTHER BOOKS BY THE AUTHOR

POETRY

Ars Poetica Chemistrica
Comment Card
Human Engine at Dawn
Gun/Shy
The Middle Ages
Street Calligraphy
Apology to the Moon
All of the Above
Rowing Inland
Birth Marks
Digger's Blues
Having a Little Talk with Capital P Poetry
Now Showing
In Line for the Exterminator
Revolt of the Crash-Test Dummies
Black Vinyl, Red Vinyl
Show and Tell: New and Selected Poems
Night with Drive-By Shooting Stars
Blue Jesus
Hacking It
Blessing the House
Greatest Hits
Niagara Falls
M-80
Punching Out
Places/Everyone
Digger's Territory
The Long Ball
On the Line
Factory Poems

FICTION

The Luck of the Fall
The Perp Walk
Eight Mile High
Trigger Man: More Tales of the Motor City
Mr. Pleasant
Detroit Tales
No Pets

NONFICTION

An Ignorance of Trees

Late Invocation for Magic

New and Selected Poems

Jim Daniels

MICHIGAN STATE UNIVERSITY PRESS | *East Lansing*

Michigan State University Press
East Lansing, Michigan 48823-5245

Library of Congress Cataloging-in-Publication Data is available.
ISBN 978-1-61186-574-5 (paperback)
ISBN 978-1-60917-828-4 (PDF)
ISBN 978-1-62895-578-1 (ePub)

Cover design by David Drummond, Salamander Design, www.salamanderhill.com

---

Visit Michigan State University Press at www.msupress.org

Contents

MegaEverything

Acknowledgments

Thank you to the publishers who originally published some of these poems in the following books and chapbooks:

BOA Editions: *Birth Marks*, 2013

Carnegie Mellon University Press: *Having a Little Talk with Capital P Poetry*, 2011; *Comment Card*, 2024

Eastern Washington University Press: *Revolt of the Crash-Test Dummies*, 2007

Red Mountain Press: *The Middle Ages*, 2018

Steel Toe Books: *Street Calligraphy*, 2017

Wayne State University Press: *Gun/Shy*, 2021; *Rowing Inland*, 2017; *In Line for the Exterminator*, 2007

Wolfson Press: *The Human Engine at Dawn*, 2022

BatCat Press: *Apology to the Moon*, 2015

Thank you to the editors of the journals in which the new poems first appeared:

Asheville Poetry Review: "Hard Crust"

Cottonwood Review: "Catholic"

Hamilton Stone: "Nightmare of My Last Class Before Retirement"

Hampden-Sydney Review: "Obedience School"

Hiram Poetry Review: "Eclipse"

Midwest Review: "Homeless Suite"

Plume: "The Bullseye of Depression," "Rowing Through the Ashes," "Dusk," "Dinner at Lynn and Linda's with Ken and Jack"

Poetry: "Tunnel to Canada"

Rattle: "French Omelet"

San Pedro River Review: "At 95"

Slant: "Living Without a Horse"

swamp pink: "Shadow of a Doubt," "The Yellow Cave"

Vox Populi: "Strawberry," "If a poem is a house"

Thank you to the National Endowment for the Arts and the Pennsylvania Council on the Arts for the fellowships during which many of these poems were written.

Thank you to former United States poet laureates for featuring the following poems:

Ted Kooser for reprinting "Brushing teeth with my sister after the wake," "Talking About the Day," and "Dim" in *American Life in Poetry*, a newspaper column sponsored by the Library of Congress and the Poetry Foundation.

Tracy K. Smith for selecting "Hair on Fire," for *The Slowdown with Tracy K. Smith*, sponsored by the Poetry Foundation and the Library of Congress.

Billy Collins for including "American Cheese" in his *Poetry 180* project.

Thank you to Garrison Keillor for featuring a number of these poems on *The Writer's Almanac*.

Thank you to *Poetry Daily* for featuring "Ode to a Reel Mower."

Thank you to *Verse Daily* for featuring "Gospel," "Poetica No Apologia Arte Kumbaya," and "Hair on Fire."

Thank you to George Bilgere for featuring "American Cheese" in his poetry newsletter, *Poetry Town*.

NOTE

Rather than group the poems by the books in which the poems first appeared, they are grouped into thematic sections.

Turning Down the Ars Poetica, Heating Up the Leftovers

Turning Down the Ars Poetica, Heating Up the Leftovers

Somewhere, a man arrives home from work
in streetlight darkness, car door etching itself

on the street's silence. Inside, leftovers on the stove.
A woman in her robe prepares his plate.

Five children asleep, radio tuned to talk
on health and home improvements and religion

though it's just soft static now as she sits down
to watch him eat, as he sits down to hear

what he missed.
I can't tell you whether they even hug or kiss

before collapsing into bed together,
for I am already in dream's tender arms.

And if this violates point of view
or logic, she'll get you a plate

and explain it all to you,
my mother.

My father worked 800 hours of overtime

on the line at Ford's the year I turned 16
and had sex with a substitute teacher
and began drinking in earnest
and selling nickel bags
out of the basement beanbag chair.

800 equals 20 extra 40-hour weeks.
Using the math invented by the State
of Michigan to lower the drinking age
to 18, that gave me 20 more hours
at the gates of oblivion.

Oblivion was a mirage state
between Michigan and Ohio.
You had to close your eyes
and pick an exit off of I-75.
Oblivion had no gates.

My father quit smoking
after three friends from work
died in a six-month span.
The cartons of Marlboros
disappeared from the closet

leaving me to my own devices
of retail theft and cadging. I couldn't
smoke my mother's Kools—
menthol was for girls. She could
either quit smoking or leave

my father. Story problems
like crickets in the basement,
mice in the kitchen, rats in the trash,
untranslatable and breeding
with the frenzy of ex-smokers.

Working at the same plant, I never
approached his record or even called to it
from a distance. I drove south on I-75
and almost approached Canada
before swerving toward Ohio, speeding

right through the mirage of my own
future, 800 hours away. Getting high
in Marlboro Country, spooking the horses,
stampeding them into stalled rust buckets
abandoned on the I-75 service drive.

I ended up in the middle of a funeral
procession heading out to a distant cemetery
where an actuary handed me a ticket
and offered condolences. Father,
I imagine you tallying up those hours,

in lieu of love, in lieu of vacation, in lieu
of even mowing the damn lawn, throwing
an extra buck in the church envelopes resting
in their box next to the coffin of Kools.
God and overtime. Abandoning

the Usher's Club and Holy Name Society
to give your reluctant work-ship to the hymns
of Henry Ford who hated Jews, loved money,
and went camping with Thomas Edison,
where they rubbed two workers together

to start their fire. My father as match head.
800 hours. His hobby? Staying alive.
Stranded in the rush hour of his own life.
Laws were broken. Canada was avoided.
Detroit, the only place in the US north

of Canada. Some nights I waited up for him
in the dark house, then ran to bed, escaping
his headlights' glare. Some nights I was out
and had to sneak back in, waiting for him
to finish his solitary beer in the yellow kitchen

while finishing my own, parked out front
in my Plymouth Satellite in the darkness
of the busted streetlight. I missed the smell
of Marlboros when he quit, the comfort
of ash, the burn that meant he'd been there.

Ankle Beach, Lake Huron

We stumbled over stones at Ankle Beach—
so named by my oldest brother. Our grandfather only
let us wade—he could not swim and save us.

We couldn't see across the cold blue to Canada
or even imagine it. Why tease us with all
that water, stuck on the shore at Ankle Beach?

He never told us about his son/our uncle who died at fifteen
when his appendix burst. Years later, a stranger did.
All we knew was Grandpa would not swim and save us.

He thrilled at freighters in the distance, wondering what
they carried, where they were going while he stood anchored.
My father kept the secret, his face a flat stone at Ankle Beach.

Grandpa's shack sat safely back, a half mile from the beach.
Silver insulation between studs reflected where he stopped
his hammering. He could not swim nor save. Us?

Lying in bed, we heard night waves crashing against shore.
Icy water numbed us with God's silence. Grandpa
watched us heave rocks into the lake at Ankle Beach,
the heavier the better. He could not swim. Save us.

Cutwoman in the Corner House

My mother the nurse, the designated secret
sharer for women in flight, angling across
the lined, square grid of streets built by men.

Mrs. Anders wobbled bruised over the back fence,
Mrs. Blondell and the glass shard, Mrs. Laney
and the teeth, Mrs. Dodge and the burn—
my mother held ice against sobs.

If women in trouble emitted contrails,
the signals quickly dissipated, wind gusted,
dogs howled, husbands hammered and cursed,
red crosses scrawled in invisible ink, shades yanked down.

The ice cream man, the sirens, the drunken hours.
My brothers and sisters pressed against the closed
kitchen door, our father at the factory, our TV ignited
for warmth—'60s situations without comedy.

The high-pitched alarm only women could hear
at our kitchen table between rounds—
what my mother did, forever dissipated. All we knew:
she patched them up, sent them home.

High School Diploma, 1917

Marie Cogan, my grandmother, lost
two children within two years. Balancing
on a wobbly footstool imported from Ireland,
she scrubbed her walls clean of them, then never
cleaned again. Marie Cogan lied about her age
until the past hazed over into truth. The one child left
conceded to the ghosts, left home and became
my father. Marie Cogan brushed my sister's hair
with the violence of a true believer and took communion
for superstitious reasons. Marie Cogan played cards
with neighbor ladies and collected music boxes,
though eventually lost her false teeth and believed
I was a doctor come to save her. She took her diploma
to the home where it hung above her bed, alone
without photographs: *Marie Cogan*, in stately scrawl
enlarged by pride—few girls finished. Not one careless
scrap of her dead children in the stinging white
of her tiny shared room, lit by music boxes
and the stench of dying. My grandfather, entering late
through the back door of their rotting wood-frame house,
takes off his work shoes and hat, washes up at the sink,
and heads to his own cold room in the back. He quit school
to work at Packard's, lying about his age, then had to lie
again, pretending to take the day off to sign up for the draft—
the only lies he ever told, except the ones of omission,
as far as I know, I, who carried both their caskets
and laid them into the earth next to the graves
of those two children, brushing away dirt from flat stones
carved with the names never spoken except haltingly,
once, by my father. *Marie Cogan*, the priest intoned.
She lived her whole life in one house until she could
no longer. *Marie Cogan*. I will sing her name
in the Old English script. Holy Redeemer High School,
have mercy on us all.

Nursing the Wounds

My mother walked to work
in her nurse's uniform—
white cap proudly pinned
over her bouffant—

down the dirt path through
the field behind Arco Tool & Die,
a narrow strip of weeds
someone forgot to develop

between 8 Mile and the cinderblock
wall where our subdivision began.
The only nurse any of us knew
in the foaming sea of housewives

calling to their schools of gritty kids
hiding in those weeds.
The only ones who wore hats
anywhere near that odd

were the troop of nuns at the convent
across from the Dairy Queen
shrunk into their black habits
that hid everything.

Her hat, a giant bleached butterfly
twisted and starched into place.
If you were to see her striding
down 8 Mile Road in white everything

toward the clinic next to Stan's Party Store
you might have paused at the mirage
emerging through the green sprawl
with the confident pace

of a woman getting a paycheck,
leaving five kids behind
to be watched by her mother.
Oh, she didn't make much,

I know now, like I know now
that the hoots and whistles
from passing cars were not due
to her angelic aura.

My mother with her own stethoscope
tucked into a straw purse like a diamond
necklace, not a blessed rosary—
though she had one or two of those.

Her laugh cut with cigarettes
and kindness and beer. What happened
at work, we never knew. All she had
for us were band-aids in her pockets

and Dum-Dums they gave to kids
who did not cry. Once riding my bike
to Stan's after delivering my newspapers
I saw her heading to work at the clinic

that needed no proper name—to cover
for a nurse out getting divorced
I learned later—I saw her skip
over the imbalanced sidewalk

in front of Steve's Service Station
where I'd later learn how to pump
gas and fix a flat. She did
a little move in the air

that involved hips and hands
in some ecstatic recreation
of something no nun was allowed
to recreate. I may have flushed

or pedaled harder to make the turn
onto Toepfer past the trailer park
so she would not see me seeing her,
skipping over the unseen past,

the abuse she never spoke of.
Memory, that unreliable friend
that whispered her troubles
to the wind, nearly unpinning

the shelter of that cap, despite
a lifetime of hearing hearts beat—
all those deep breaths we took
while she listened.

One Word

My brother lies in his hospital bed
steeped in the clammy smell
of the almost-dead. Stitches hang
stiff under his chin, a scraggly
Fu Manchu they sewed on him
fresh off Life Flight, his motorcycle
mangled by a sixteen-year-old
running a stop sign. My brother
is simply trying to speak. To push out
a single word. The breathing tube's
been removed—we thought when it came out
he'd be telling us he's going to be alright
or at least where it hurts. But the brain rattle's
sent him spinning, woven a fuzzy web around him.
We're bent over, smelling the pain, at his lips, so close
those stitches prick. *What? Listen. C'mon, try again—*
it's more than a groan and less than satisfactory.
Like the slo-mo grunt of a tennis player so jazzed up
they can't just hit it and keep quiet. Like the door
to the principal's office swinging open
for you. More than a squeak and less
than adequate. *C'mon, open your eyes.*
Just one eye. A sound like grating bread crumbs.
An oral afterthought unfinished.
The chair you can't get comfortable in.
A dud firework. Six days, and they haven't given him
a bath—he reeks. His thing's beeping again
and where's the nurse and—wait, he's trying again—
we love you, can you hear us? It's less than a whistle
and more than maddening. The Tin Man's rusted
whispers, his faux clumsy rattling dance—that dude's
going to Oz, so why not us? We all of us have hearts.
Brother, we'll make a deal with the damn witch,
trade her some of your neat handwriting
and good manners—broomstick, slippers—a package deal
for a little translation, a little more wet space

between the dry lips for sound to slip out—anything,
anything, my eyes closed, concentrating on the subtle rise
and fall of what are less than syllables
but more than random. Oh, my brother,
we're lighting the torches and heading out into the darkness
to find the words and bring them back to you.

Family Relic: The Suicide Policeman's Blackjack

I look for bloodstains in the leather weapon
like I looked for Lincoln's in the chair
from Ford's Theater displayed in Greenfield Village
imagining the moment of impact.

He killed himself with *his service revolver*,
the tiny brittle clipping reads.
Small enough to miss in the daily paper,
but someone didn't.

My great uncle. I got his watch fixed.
Won for racing pigeons, it hangs
on its ceremonial hook as if waiting
to hypnotize the naïve or compassionate.

The blackjack, the clipping, the watch.
You might think it's a mysterious triangle,
but we follow dotted lines, jump over the gaps
in the liquored pools of our besotted history.

*

My father enters the frame
turns the scrapbook page
fingers the blackjack
whacks the loose ball bearings
in their dry leather sack against his palm,
another way we keep time
in our family

and I'm hearing shot glasses
clocking against the wooden table
in a rhythmic dirge
some might blame on blood

so who did he hit and when,
and why are there no survivors

to smudge these pages,
to fill in and erase and reinvent,
to claim the clock,
to claim the blackjack
and its history of hitting?

*

I stared at the leather chair
roped off from my grasp
and imagined the dark, stuffy theater
and the enormous Lincoln of history books.

I listen to my father enumerate the victims
of the curse that runs—does not walk
or stroll or jog or mosey—in the family.
The particulars, I imagine.

The bedtime story I half-told myself
during my own drunken years—
good uncles, half cousins, great aunts,
laughter cut short, clock hands woozy.

We changed the spelling of our name
and the labels on our bottles.
We hid the weapons and the maps.
The keys and the locks.

*

My father flutters the pages
and I hear the wings
of pigeons, the dirty birds
of our heritage.
By his own hand. Somewhere
a steady hand fixed the clock
while cruelty landed its blows
and my father taught me

not to turn away
  but to witness
        and pass on.

The blackjack in a box
  will be mine,
the rhythm section to the song
  I sing to my children
and the small dogs of their dreams
  that do not bark or bite.
About the birds who come home to roost
  and how we shoo them away
by all means necessary.
  About how I define survival
as avoiding small hard things and reading
  the small print, and telling time
the old-fashioned way.

Company Men

My grandfather worked at Packard's for 43 years.
My father worked at Ford's for 35.
One brother worked at Big Boy for 20
then Chrysler's for 15 and counting. Another
worked at GE for 35 and counting.
The third worked at Chevron for 30
and counting. I worked at Carnegie Mellon for 32
and counting and counting.

We do not look for new jobs.
We take what they give us. We drink our coffee
black. We tip the mailman at Christmas. We mow
our lawns and prop up our homes, reluctant
to call an electrician or plumber. We believe in
fixing what's broke. Not in cafeteria lines or IOUs.
We pack our own lunches. We are proud of taking it
without complaint.

We believe in God's dance floor
and the boogie-woogie of interest-
bearing checking accounts.
We accept wooden nickels
and trim them into five toothpicks.
We like toothpicks. If a restaurant offers none,
we are permanently suspicious. We fly our flags
on holidays but not bumper stickers. We do not
believe in bumper stickers of any kind.
We believe in Turtle Wax and in all things turtle
because we are plodding in our hard shells
toward the finish line.

When Packard's went belly up, my grandfather lost
his pension. He lived off social security
for thirty more years. He handed out dollar bills
to his grandsons like tickets to the big game
he was unable to go to himself

due to prior commitments. And we took
those dollar bills and saved them
for rainy days, for it was always a sunny day
when we got dollars from our grandfather.

Nobody has a gold watch. But we will tell you
the time. And if we are stupidly smug
about our years of seniority, forgetting
the lesson of our grandfather, forgive us.
We are not squeaky wheels. We are silent
even on each other's porches, analyzing mortar
between bricks for signs of crumbling.

Our companies moved us up
then stopped moving us up.
So we listen to the young bucks
and nod as they tell us how to do our jobs.
We do not discuss our jobs.
We leave our jobs where they belong.

Two of us laid off now, counting suspended
due to inclement weather or unreliable mathematicians,
a wrong turn or global high jinks, we can't be sure,
rubbing our fingers across the mortar.

The story says the tortoise beat the hare,
but that's not what our bank books say.
We are never late, God willing—
though we're not sure he is.

American Dream

Some of the jobs these machines replaced were difficult, boring, or dangerous; others were good jobs that paid well and workers enjoyed.
—Robotics exhibit, Henry Ford Museum, Dearborn, Michigan

My father, my children, my wife, and I
were recruited to work on a toy car assembly-line.
My son placed the yellow plastic frame onto
the conveyor. My wife snapped the red body onto
the frame. My father snapped the blue seats in.
I pushed the front end on. My daughter cranked
the conveyor, controlling the speed. We each had
a small box of parts. The museum employee
in her perky red vest started a Chaplinesque sound track,
and we began, working smoothly till she instructed my daughter
to crank faster, and we got backed up, tossing half-
formed cars to the side. *Faster,* she kept telling her.
We ran out of parts just as the music stopped. The employee
counted good cars and bad. Bad outnumbered good. My son
asked if we could keep the cars. She said, *No*—in fact,
we had to take them apart, so that others could put them
together again. My father and I had worked on assembly lines
where if you couldn't keep up, you were fired.
Where time controllers assessed how long each job
should take and set the line speed. The family
that took our places asked me to videotape the whole thing.
I wish I could say I was making this up. Inside, I felt
the old humiliation throbbing again in my stooped back.
I told this woman bossing my daughter around
I wanted to see my union rep—as a kind of joke
but not. She had a script to stick to, and probably
made minimum wage herself. She didn't explain
to us what we were supposed to take away
from our experience. Just not the cars.

Today my bank sent me a birthday message

and spelled Happy with three a's.

It said *to the one and only James.*
It said *Hooray.* And *get the party started.*

My mother was sleeping when I called
to wish that she might wish me

a happy birthday. Hospice had just left.
When she is sleeping, you do not

wake her. She never spelled words
with extra letters to try and be some-

one more hip in her neat measured
script I'll never see again. Once, we

combined our cash into a CD when the rate
was over 10%. Free china, too, and she let me

keep it all. Her new medicine causes
constipation, so they gave her a laxative.

My father, 91, fumbles for the word
laxative. Everyone tries to make her

comfortable. Last time she was lucid,
she offered to give my daughter some cash

for a trip she's taking. She says she still has
some. My mother wants to go with her.

Semi-lucid. As good as it gets. A blessing
and curse, lucidity. I've got a million phrases

to toss over the phone lines to keep static at bay.
She is blind. We see. We are all waiting.

It's your special day that's all about you,
the bank says. They no longer give away dishes.

A whole stack of those silver-rimmed plates
once tipped out of my cabinet and smashed

on the floor. I still have the smaller plates,
and the shallow bowls that are frankly

the wrong size for anything. Plus,
not microwave safe. My father fashioned

braille buttons on the microwave for her
at an earlier point in her demise. She

is failing. Dying. We call it many things.
Got a birthday check in your pocket?

The bank asks. There are many *Jameses*
in this ill-formed world. When I used to call,

back in the great state of Clarity, she'd ask,
Is this the famous James Raymond Daniels?

A joke between us—I've always been Jim
and obscure. I will call again tomorrow

when she is awake and it's no longer
my birthday. I believe she will be alive.

I will never see her again. She has not
seen me for years. These last days, she is not

even one-A Happy. Interest rates went down,
as everybody knows. Why am I so certain?

Maybe I should make the drive one more time
to hold her hand and play along with the script-

less prayers. My father talks about a D-Day
special on TV. New footage of the blood

and horror from other countries put together
with our bloody American footage. All

for my birthday. Blood and money together.
He calls me Jimmy. The bank wants to know

if I'm *running low on celebration cash*. Oh, bank,
I want to say, but it says DoNotReply.

To protect my privacy some pictures in the message
have not been downloaded. I download confetti

and a birthday cupcake. It looks like bran
or gingerbread, a swirl of frosting on top

and a candle photoshopped into lit. Bank,
my mother would have told you I want

devil's food for my birthday. Bank,
why are you such a bummer on my birthday?

Party on. Keep the fun going. © Bank,
I'm not very Haaappy. The cupcake floats

in white space. It would sit nicely
on one of those small plates.

My mother says DoNotReply today.
Thin as a candle, burned down

to nearly nothing.
I dare not blow.

Obedience School

Near the end, the experts on loss
sold us a robot dog that barked
and leaned into the touch

to give comfort to my blind dying
mother. She wasn't fooled enough
to name it—or *gone* enough,

though she was pretty gone
then. We put it in her hands
and she stroked it

then hurled it across the room.
Nothing to lose is never true.
Always something more to lose.

I turned the dog off.
Bad dog, I said.

Strawberry

The final time I saw my mother
she was trying to find
the last strawberry on her plate.
I walked up behind her

and kissed the top of her head
and said *I love you*. She reached
up a sticky hand and brushed
away where I kissed

then lowered it again
into the juicy bowl. I was going
to say we never know which
strawberry will be our last

but I think she knew—
damn slippery thing.

Brushing teeth with my sister after the wake

at my kitchen sink, the bathroom upstairs
clogged with family from out of town

spending the night after the wake
and the after-wake—cold beverages

have been consumed and comfort food,
leftovers bulging both the fridge

and the mini fridge. In our sixties, both
half-asleep half-awake, we face each

other. My sister's smile foams white
down her chin at the end of a day

on which no one has smiled. We laugh.
We may never brush our teeth together again.

No mirror down here to see our haggard faces.
We rinse, we spit. As we were taught.

French Omelet

When my parents came to France to visit
they got on the wrong train. We lived
in the middle of nowhere, too small
for their map. We retrieved them

at another station and drove to our small
house surrounded by someone else's
grape vines. My father, retired from Ford's
in Detroit, could not believe how narrow

the roads were—unmarked paths,
two-way traffic on one lane, requiring
small gestures of deference. On leave,
I had a small break from marking

papers. My mother had raised five kids
and nursed her tiny mother till she died.
All she wanted was a French omelet.
Out of season, the small restaurants

nearby were closed. I myself did not know
what made an omelet French. We grew
up with scrambled eggs on special
occasions and hard-boiled at Easter.

My two small children liked sweet brioche
toasted for breakfast in our dark, stony kitchen.
My mother read them bedtime stories.
My father built fires in the fireplace.

We were all in some version of heaven
though my mother already relied
on a cane and wore tinted glasses
on the narrowing road to a wheelchair

and blindness. She got her omelet
in a roadside café one sunny February
afternoon warm enough to sit out
on the tiny terrace. She refused to be

disappointed with their small, modest
lives, their ordinary children.
She was in France! Eating an omelet!
So light she had to keep it from floating

away with her fork. Just the five of us
in the café. My father could relax
now that she had her omelet.

We squinted into the sun with all
the time in the world as the clocks
briefly paused to grant her that small wish.
I keep saying small even as it grows

in memory, looming down
from the distant sky years after
her passing. I can see that full
yellow plate in front of her.

She ate it for the rest of her life.

My father anxiously awaits the delivery of the new mattresses

for the guest room his children refer to
as The Penthouse, the one room upstairs
in the condo he and my mother moved to
in their eighties and that she died in
11 months ago, and her room remains
untouched downstairs, her ashes in the closet
along with dresses bought but barely
worn and somebody should want them
he says, reluctant to go to Goodwill—
nobody in the family wants them
though his grandson's wife took away
the treadmill they called the walking machine
out of the basement after the accident
when he'd turned it off, forgetting she was blind   oh

my brother prepaid for the mattresses
and my father worries they'll never
deliver, that my brother might be *a chump!*
And who's paying for it? Me!
And what's wrong with those old mattresses
from ancient Rome—ancient Rome, the street
we grew up on, two bunk beds in one room, four boys   oh

if those stains could talk!
11 months ago, I went to say goodbye
but just managed to get hello in—
I stood in the kitchen trying to say
my last farewell while she concentrated
on one fat strawberry in the bowl—
she was giving it a ride with her spoon
but it wouldn't climb aboard
so her fingers dipped in and well   oh

you know strawberries—slippery!
Fingers and face and juicy red juice
as if she were—well, she was
dying in her wheelchair
listing to one side as if the wind
or waves were tilting the boat
and I managed to kiss the top
of her head before she tipped over
into the deep deep sea   oh

they took away the hospital bed
pretty damn fast
and the wheelchair
and whatever else Medicare
and hospice provided
no one mentioning the lumpy
mattresses upstairs
the walls decorated
with plastic beer signs
from the store 3 of us
had worked at   oh

the hangovers on those beds
the spinning—imagining
we were falling overboard
down to the cold cement
basement floor of the bunk room
plywood two-by-fours and a toilet
the opposite of a penthouse
space heater night-glow
dehumidifier water dumped
into the washtub every day
Daddy-   oh

where are those mattresses
they better be nice for what he paid
how can you order mattresses
on a computer anyway?
you can't feel them first
you can't fall back on them
and who knows when you'll
be eating your last strawberry   oh

at 92 he sits at the kitchen table
and pays the bills by check
and even he can hear
the clock ticking now
the shedding of sound
the stripping of sheets
they wheeled the bed
out the door along with
her last breath, and I could
be standing there still
waiting for her attention
a proper goodbye
the five-hour drive
ahead of me/behind me
the illegal turnpike
U-turn the doubled toll
at the booth
she died on Feb 29
leap day   oh
not even listed on this year's
giant calendar where he marks
his memory in the empty boxes
while in the cold unheated bedroom
down the hall the ashes wait
for his, so they can go in
the vault together
like a king and queen

at the two-for-one rate
checkbook balanced
as he rows alone
the narrowing river

oh

At 95

My father set the table for breakfast
after spending the night hearing voices.

He said they sound like a preacher
in the rhythm of a sermon

but he cannot decipher the words.
In from out of town, here to try

to scare away the voices. If only I too
could hear them. He's been waiting

for me in the kitchen, his sleepless face
buried in his hands. He's tried to give me

his suitcase, saying he'll never need it again.
We watch rain spill over his clogged gutters.

I stir my spoon in an empty cup.

Street Calligraphy

Street Calligraphy

Shingles blown from roofs or spacers pried
from between concrete slabs
lasted longer than chalk but not forever.

Chalk was school. Nobody used
chalk. Plaster worked, cracked drywall
heaped for trash. We dusted its edges
against concrete in gritty, deliberate scrawl.

What we lacked in depth
we made up for with blatant lies
or cruel wishes: *Eats Shit. Sucks Dick.*

The truth was off its hinges
or hidden in the blind spot
the world had for us, somewhere
beyond mirrors or jewelry.

Nothing harder than concrete.
Certainly not our skin. Certainly not glass.
I stashed shingles and plaster
beneath a broken brick in a field of weeds.

We marked out narrow diamonds, baselines
squeezed into the choked vein of our street.
The only fair balls shot right down the middle
then rolled and rolled, coming to rest
under parked cars or against far curbs.

Our balls were taped or rubber, our bats
plastic, or cracked and nailed. Our mitts
theoretical. We drew yard markers, end zones.
Cars served as both obstacle and blocker.
Ricochet passes off windshields? Ruled complete.

Leaked oil and antifreeze marked parking spots.
The cruel whimsy of Safe-T-Glass lay sprinkled
against the curb like the dice of large insects
or small rodents. We had no tears, and nothing
with which to make tears.

Don't get me wrong, I wish we had tears.
To dilute the street, drain anger,
erase bitterness, erode the fist.
Tar blackened our fingers, sticky
in summer, as we drew dark lines,

stick men, designed for crude cursing,
pure permanent wobble. We came equipped
to trash each other. Short-witted, dim-sighted,
prone to slamming on brakes, leaving
the rubber lines of our near misses.

Down the empty eyes of manhole covers
we shoved our true messages—
unread in their dark falling disappearance.

I wrote, FIND ME on a scrap of paper
with a nub of bitten pencil. Alone on the curb,
I sat watching rain darken cement
till all dots connected.

It smelled like our lives then, the damp glisten
of time, the baited shove toward our futures.
Tar—tell me anything before the torn slice of roof
disintegrates into an articulate mirage.

Our street, a book permanently open
to the same two pages.
Demanding to be memorized.

The Religious Significance of the Super Ball

The Super Ball was invented in 1965. Thrown down, it could leap over a three-story building . . . and would bounce on for about a minute after being dropped from a short distance. Wham-O's oft-repeated claim was that the ball had 92 percent resiliency.

My brother and I drank in the kitchen while the adults drank
in the basement. We'd lifted a twelve-pack from the fridge.
No one noticed or cared. Somebody called to offer condolences
and I laughed till beer spewed out my nose.

What was funny about my grandmother dying?
She'd lived with us for fifteen years. We should've been . . . what?
Drinking with our parents instead? Her children, reunited members
of the unacknowledged "A" team of alcohol. Ten more years
and two more funerals before anyone tacked on the other A.

*

My grandmother only drank Drambuie, and only for medicinal
purposes. Downstairs, they passed a bottle in her memory.
A cousin's pocket bulged with a Super Ball.
They'd just come out, replacing the Slinky in Fadville.

We took the kid outside into the March thaw. *Grandma farts a lot,*
he said. He didn't live with her. He thought she still might be
coming back. We held him down, dislodged it from
his sticky hands. We hammered his Super Ball
against the street bearded with dirty snow
and watched it disappear.

*

That chubby little cousin killed himself twenty years later.
Too much dessert. Eat your vegetables, dude,
I should've said. It bounced high and wild, ricocheting
off the parked cars of the grieving. Cold enough

for runny noses, the back of a sleeve. Good burn in the lungs.
Nobody wore coats. Nobody had any dope. Big bust
in the neighborhood. We lost the damn ball—kid started bawling.
We drove off in Grandma's car—an old brown Buick with no radio—

to the five-and-dime and bought a bunch of Super Balls
with cash stolen from the funeral kitty. The kid was happy.
Everybody was happy. A Super Ball Orgy. My brother and I
stood at each end of the block, firing them back and forth

watching them rise over our boxy little houses till it got dark
or we ran out of beer or got cold or somebody barked us back
into the wake to move the ping-pong table or drive Aunt Millie home.

*

It's okay to laugh. Aunt Millie'd caught us. *Cool, Aunt Millie—*
did you ever get high? Got any dope?
Grandma liked the Irish Rovers. I was taking requests,
cranking up "Danny Boy" at 45 rpm till it almost rocked.

We bought Grandma a new rosary each year.
Blessed by the pope. Touched by the kids in Guadalupe.
Made by blind mice in Omaha. She left each of us one.
They jiggled in our pockets like Chiclets, the cross,

a crotch discomfort. I don't know how Grandma
would've wanted to go, but not as Farting Grandma.
Where'd everybody go? Just me and my brother
at the kitchen table, into the Drambuie ourselves,
sick with memory.

*

I'd loved her, little old Grandma, but I was
a Stupor Ball. Jesus was her Super Ball.
I shouldn't have been driving her old car.
The moon came out to shame me.

Fifteen years of her shrinking, reduced
resiliency, curling into herself with the fragile
delicacy of a charcoal snake till she disintegrated
and blew away. So, get mad, get drunk, laugh loud.

Drinking as hobby, sport, part-time job. As she went deaf,
silence leaked from her bones. She must've believed
she was coming back to Jesus, bead by bead.
Nobody had funny stories to tell about her.

Watching the Super Balls erupt off cement
in a reckless, indestructible surge, I became addicted too,
and shame on me. 92% resiliency.
I wound up and smashed my grief into concrete,
but it simply rose and rose, high, higher still.

Up on Blocks

His father limping
from his stroke
heaving his lunch pail
into the back of his pickup
like some stubborn, gimpy
shot putter, then driving off
to the job they gave him
after his rehab: steering
a Hi-Lo through the greasy plant

after Danny died

one day recovering on the porch
he hollered for the ice cream man
to stop, then bought us all popsicles

after Danny died

because his son—Vietnam—and so, and so
he had a cough that could maul a lion
but he wouldn't stop smoking

after Danny died

Danny left his car, an absurdly red
Fury, up on blocks on our pocked street
to work on when he got home
but he never did, so

after Danny died

the car sat rusting—
no one touched it for years
till one night some asshole torched it
a whoosh heard down the block

and his father trembled and collapsed
in the terrible light of the flames

after Danny died

a tow truck dragged away the mess
gouging concrete into sparks as it pulled away
leaving charred cinderblocks like used-up Bibles,
and we hauled them away to the weedy field
behind Bronco Lanes where they may be lying still

after Danny died

oh, the shame of the unmarked grave
somewhere off the end of our radio dials
while we fiddled with the blown fuses
of our cheap electric hearts

after Danny died

his father survived the second stroke
with one arm twitching and returned to sit
on that porch, drooling odd noises,
flinging his good arm at flies, and I sat with him
one afternoon for hours, then never again

after Danny died

because I was no saint and he was no prophet
and his pickup replaced the Fury
as the vehicle going nowhere
and his wife bagged groceries at the A&P
down the block and brought home
what she could carry

after Danny died

and we were fierce and serious boys
who would never go to war and thus
could always be fierce, and we too
smoked cigarettes and swore
and fucked and carried on like Danny did

before he died

and I have not mentioned his stoic bride
and the ramshackle wedding of a false
pregnancy annulled shortly after
but he had already signed up
that's the way it was on our street
of the hard luck and the harder

before and after Danny died

and he planted a bottle of Boone's Farm
on every table in the grade school cafeteria
and we squeezed onto the tiny benches
and danced to Top 40 in front of the stage
where the bridal party sat

and he guzzled from the bottle
like the king of America
in his frilly tuxedo shirt,
and his father—Lord, his name
was Branko—gave the saddest
toast I'd ever heard, then sat down
and smiled the beatific smile
of the damned and the oblivious

and I cannot remember it now
having drunk from the bottle myself
at fifteen—nobody fought, and he left happy,
and the bride and groom drove off in the Fury
toward the welcoming cliff and

after Danny died

the war ended quickly, and the ice cream man
got busted for selling drugs

we all stood at attention
at Branko's funeral
like soldiers who had lost their general

because he had once bought us popsicles
because we would live forever

and no one burned the pickup
and his widow took to driving it
and one winter morning
I scraped her windows clear
then never again

after Danny died

because I had my own car, and it started
and ran, and I put on as many miles as I could

after Danny died.

Rowing Inland

On the only vacation of my childhood
we followed the Detroit legend of "Great Lakes,
Great Times" up the gridlock of I-75 to a cottage
in the great holy expanse called Up North.

On Tea Lake, where I never saw anyone drink tea
or discuss tea, or remark that the color of the lake
resembled tea, we rented one of the dilapidated shacks
owned by a cousin of our neighbor Branko

and referred to without irony as a resort.
I was rib-boned skinny at ten, and Kim,
Branko's daughter, was nine, blonde hair
bleached by that bright young sun.

Our parents drank beer and smoked cigarettes
as always—but longer, with more savor—
in splintery chairs on the splintery dock.
Our fathers discussed fishing but did no fishing.

They shouted to those in rowboats,
how's the fishing? but they did no fishing.
I only faintly began to realize life
was mostly a series of rhetorical questions:

Hot enough for you? Working hard,
or hardly working? Our fathers carried
identical black lunch buckets each morning
to different locations linked by the same underground

tunnel of machinery and grease and one giant time clock
registering the equation of the city's heartbeat
divided by the number of new cars built that year.
Our mothers discussed other mothers and swore

off cooking for a week, swore like they never did
at home. *Shit*, they sighed, *shit*, echoing out over
calm water. Straps on bathing suits hung loose.
They painted their nails because they could.

They lost track of their children. Kim and I sat
in a rotting wooden rowboat on the weedy shore.
We donned faded orange life vests
and placed oars in locks and rowed

through sand and air, calling *stroke, stroke*
like we'd seen in a cartoon about a dog.
We never laughed at cartoons—no one
ever really got hurt. No TV at Tea Lake.

Coffee and beer. We were allowed orange drink
in paper cartons, and potato chips galore.
Left alone, we caught fireflies and poison ivy,
mosquito bites and berries, and firecrackers

from the bad kid down the road who spat
with alarming accuracy. We waded in shallow water,
screwing our feet into cold muck. Roads were dirt,
and street signs nonexistent. We carved our names

on white birch bark and imagined
we had the bravery and stealth of scouts.
After a week, we were back on the grid
of our shallow street, riding the banks of curbs

on our bikes and setting ants on fire.
If you look at anything long and hard enough,
it catches fire. Another giant clock out there:
the Tragedy Clock. No second, minute,

or hour hands. Just a big gong sounding
without warning. One stroke after another
killed her father. He called me Jimmy, limping
out of his pickup, bearing that black, metal coffin

home each day while I sat on her porch or mine.
Kim and I kissed in the realm of first and foremost,
climbing out bedroom windows when we were thirteen.
But we never went to the chapel of intercourse

and instead slipped away from each other
like embarrassed fish released back into water,
still bloody from the hook. Kim left school
and married the father of her child. It didn't sit

right with Branko. She moved away, and I didn't
see her for years. Branko held her child
in his wheelchair the last time I saw either of them.
I waved from my porch. *It's Jimmy*, I said.

Her husband—do you want me to go on,
pounding the Tragedy Clock
with my mallet? *Stroke, stroke*,
we rowed together over the shore.

Eclipse

Six children died today in a fire which swept through their home. But the oldest boy, 13, saved two brothers and himself. The children who perished were Martha Ann, 11; Mary Jo, 7 (found outside the house); John, 6; Diana, 4; James, 3, and Charles, 18 months. Mother, Marie, was taken to Holy Cross Hospital in critical condition where she died Christmas Eve. The father, Elbert Turner Cole Sr. (or *"Albert"*), *40, a steelworker, was en route home from his part-time job as a cab driver when the fire struck about 3 a.m. The boys' window was open because they had been watching an eclipse of the moon.*

The Cole boys were in our Scout troop,
#1354. Our mother carefully patched
clothes and added them to the donation
pile in the grade school gym.

Christmas. News teams absurdly out
of place as new toys. How big a head-
line for seven dead? For years, the immoveable
touchstone for tragedy: *at least it wasn't*

like the Coles. With 9 kids, even a steelworker
needed a side job. The house, a three-bedroom box
on John B Street, identical to ours. Named
for someone who was not rich like John R

of John R Road. We'd need a lot more cash
to buy the R—a fancy street with 3 restaurants,
2 banks. We never saw those boys in our clothes.
They went back South where their father's name

was Elbert. The *Scout Handbook* told us not to look
at an eclipse of the sun. No one told us or those boys
about the moon. How many times can you tell
the same story without melting the words into a blur

or fading into guesswork or a shrug? A rumor spun
that Albert was out drinking, and perhaps
he liked his liquor like everybody else's father.
No one we knew took cabs. The mother dying

on the sidewalk was true, though how she got there
we never knew. We, us, the unidentified
neighbors in the news, passed the hellish
half-shell of house and piles of charred rubble.

School on break. The stiff denim of new jeans
turned our legs blue in wet snow. Snow neatly
shoveled and banked as if it might save us.
Our folks let us keep our jackets.

They wouldn't have left us out there
without something in December.
For years, the touchstone for freezing:
breath-smoke. Icicles of shattered words.

Three boys studied the sky
while the others died. Something
covering up something else in darkness.
Mothers hugged their kids tight

till they squirmed. Fathers checked
furnaces and stoves. They counted heads
then went back to making cars
in the new year still loaded

with short dark days. An open window
on a December night in Detroit—
what sense did it make? How hard
that old furnace worked to compensate.

I felt bad for not liking the oldest boy,
now a hero. None of us are heroes,
our father said. Our mother decided
she wanted one more, but our father

said he wasn't driving no cab.
I secretly saved the huge headlines
that daily shrunk, then disappeared.
Even now, each time the sun covers

the moon on its preordained journey
I try to remember to look up at what
the oldest saw—the moon disappearing
at 13. Sometimes I forget

busy with my own sun and moon
and everything in between.

Outdoor Chef

Nobody believes my high school
offered a class called OUTDOOR CHEF.
The yearbook carried a picture of us firing up
the barbecue in the parking lot. This was before
the Invention of the Gas Grill. Before they
raised the drinking age back to 21. Jimi Hendrix
burned his guitar at Monterey then died shortly after,
bumming us out in OUTDOOR CHEF. It was only
a one-semester course so we had to cram. Charcoal lighter
was routinely abused. We spelled our names
on the sidewalk and lit them, like pissing
in snow. Our teacher was Mrs. Reynolds. Enormous
and cheerful and in retrospect willfully ignorant and alcoholic.
It was a difficult class to teach—no textbook. Mr. Farwell,
our principal, needed higher graduation rates, courses
to shunt problem kids into. Not one fight in OUTDOOR CHEF,
despite having the toughest guys in the school bunched together
around the grills. Class was often outside, even in winter.
Class was often cut, long wild hair disappearing into snow
toward the parking lot. Joints often snaked between us,
smoke blending with burning meat. I learned a lot
about cooking chicken and pork. See, those are
important things. You can get sick not cooking
them long enough, and make others sick too.
Neighbors would never come over for a cookout again.
My apron had some crude joke about a hot dog on it.
So did everyone else's. I can't begin to express how clever
we were. We cooked a whole turkey for Thanksgiving
and served it to Mr. Farwell and Mr. Stark,
the assistant principal/hit man. He said he could've used
a course like that when he was in school. They did not get sick.
It was a festive occasion until we let a live turkey
loose in the main hallway. No girls in OUTDOOR CHEF,
though you might have guessed that. The jocks
were subdued and serious about remaining eligible.
Our school had few jocks to spare. The rest of us

were lighting each other's long hair on fire
and thinking that was a fine joke.
Okay, Eddie Bucco did get stabbed with a skewer
but we all agreed it was an accident. We enjoyed waving
our hands above the hot coals—none of us bothered
with winter gloves. The last day of class, Jackie Smoker
brought in his cheap electric guitar and tried to imitate
Hendrix blasting from his nearby car radio.
He messed up his hands bad, but for a while, it was
beautiful. Even now, I am full of self-mockery
and loathing. The truth was that for many of us
having our own barbecue would indicate
a successful life. Mrs. Reynolds had gone to college
to teach home ec. We should have treated her better. Her
and everybody else. Yes, it's on my transcript with a C—
our final had some math on it. The wind blew ash and smoke
into the air just like at the factory down the road.
We had to provide our own briquettes. There's an enormous
number of things you can cook outdoors. The only class
in which we believed what the teacher told us.
Because we could see. That, and gym.
We chewed gum outside and threw it against
the school building. Mr. Farwell gave most of us
diplomas. I don't know how many years
OUTDOOR CHEF was offered.
You could not burn your marshmallow
on the test. That, when all we wanted
was to go up in flames.

Hair on Fire

We ironed fall leaves
  between wax-paper sheets.
We melted crayons to make candles
  and froze Kool-Aid into popsicles.
We jammed cloves into oranges. We grew roots
  on sweet potatoes tooth-picked in water.
We taped our broken glasses together
  and shut up. We made shoebox
dioramas with Play-Doh and modeling clay.
  We cut snowflakes from folded paper
and hung them with kite string.
  We made newspaper kites
and imagined they could fly.

We shaped tinfoil into fake coins
  for our church envelopes.
We covered love bites with Kool-Aid.
  We filled liquor bottles with holy water.
We hid our stash in beanbag chairs.
  We drove to Ohio for drugs
and rolled back our father's odometers.
  We lay with our lovers
on basement pool tables, clacking balls together
  for ears upstairs.
We drew lies with chalk
  and the truth with tar.
We lit our hair on fire
  to cover the smell.

Calling Out Marlene Miller

She died in a freak fire—spilled gas
caught on the dryer pilot. Thirteen,
we'd been heading toward high-school cool.
If we had ants in our pants, they clustered.
We sure itched to take them off
and run naked around the block—
and did one night that summer.

Some of us already had funeral black to wear.
We dared each other to approach the coffin
like it was some super-duper high dive.
We were supposed to whisper a prayer,
but we'd just stopped praying
and weren't ready yet to start up again,
but we couldn't just say *Hey* or *See ya*.

In the parking lot, squinting through
Kools and Marlboros, we couldn't tell
funny stories about her, or look past our own
thin shadows. Fred and Andy argued
over whether the song went "God Loves Rock 'n' Roll"
or "God, Love, and Rock 'n' Roll." Bill sniffed
smelling salts he'd lifted, and his eyebrows
disappeared. Someone had switched our lives
to reverse, and we couldn't decode the secret lyrics.

Hey Marlene, remember that time you
gave me a hickie? Remember that time
I snapped your bra strap? Hey,
Marlene, remember our swollen lips
after we'd kissed all night in the empty garage?
Hey Marlene, remember that time I rode you
on my bike down to the corner store
and we ate red popsicles and laughed at
each other's clown faces and you grabbed
my waist as we rode over a bump,
how you screamed and laughed?

Hey—Marlene.

Late Invocation for Magic

In our box houses
on our cracked sidewalks
on our pockmarked streets
we scoffed at magic early on

and tormented anyone who didn't
until they sulked back into their dark
basements with their hidden-ball tricks,
their sleeves full of scarves.

We threw popcorn at the movie screens
of every kiss and happy ending.
We built plastic models of our favorite
monsters and made good use

of leftover glue. The only trick
was *here today, gone tomorrow,*
but we knew where everybody went,
the bigger box, the big black hat

of the factory no rabbits ever
emerged from. Nobody wore
a hat like that to begin with
in a neighborhood of good bullies

and bad. Our fathers cracked
their knuckles against our skulls.
It relieved tension. What was that game
where we just took turns punching

each other? The one where we jumped
randomly on one of our own
just for practice? If it's magic,
why would you have to practice?

Our fairy princes and princesses
died in fiery midnight crashes.
Our priests couldn't even get it up for Jesus,
and, thus, overcompensated.

A long time ago, yet still I'm choking
on the bitter fumes that tainted
the fancy gilt letters of faith
and any kindness not compensated

with cash. The colder and harder, the better—
the better the batter for silver dollar
pancakes at The Clock diner Sunday morning
while mass droned on down the block.

There's a trick to get a stick shift
into reverse. One drunken night
my sister and I danced in the back of a pickup
till a neighbor got out his gun and shot.

We rose from the dead rather quickly
and without ceremony or to-do. The neighbor
paused to reload, and we somersaulted
over the bushes like superheroes.

My brother bought a Jacuzzi with the settlement
from his motorcycle accident. Some teenager
ran a stop sign and sent him flying into the ER
from which he emerged much less certain

but one winter night he called me to ask
if it was snowing here too because it was
beautiful coming down on the steam
as he sat there in hot water admiring
his neighbor's controversial high fence.

Attitude, that's something we could wrap
our fists around. Takes attitude to build
a high stone fence against all codes
because you hate your neighbor.

C'mon, slap out of it. Every fairy tale
seems to end with the ogre getting his cut,
people looking back over their shoulders
even when the promised land beckons.

We drew a treasure map once, then found
something to bury. A dead dog, but we treated it
with due respect. You can't fix a magic wand
with duct tape and X-brand adhesive.

I miss those monsters—Gihdorah, Mothra,
Rodan, and the dapper master of ceremonies,
Godzilla. And, the humans—Werewolf,
Dracula, Henry Ford. I loved painting
their tiny eyeballs.

Magic, magic, I keep repeating, on the path,
following the markers, trying to get there.
All of our wands turned out to be
sharp and pointy and humorless.

The plan for this part was to be more
upbeat, to find an earned magic to believe in,
to celebrate the wispy colored scarves of dreams,
to hold hands in the street in a great kumbaya moment
or to at least stop smoking cigarettes.

The magic words were all advertising slogans
for companies that served as fronts for the mob.
Perhaps I exaggerate. We sawed each other
not in half, but down to size.

We had one girl on our street
who could sing all the high notes
and won all the talent contests.
I'll call her Marlene, though I could call

her anything now, dead these fifty years.
Use your imagination. Close your eyes
and make a wish. Say the magic words.

I Dreamt I Wrote a Poem About Jazz

I wrote *Miles, Bird, Trane*. I almost wrote *Dizzy*,
then I started thinking about Dizzy Dean,
the last thirty-game winner in the N. L., 1934.
Denny McLain went 31–6 for the Tigers in '68.
I was there when he won his thirtieth. Dizzy on hand
to offer congratulations. Young Reggie Jackson—
already the straw that spiked the drink—hit two homers
for the A's, though it was not enough. In '68,
when the wind blew in off the river, Detroit still bled
wet smoke from the uprising. We'd taken the bus downtown
for ladies/retirees day, 50 cents for kids under 12,
then scrunched down with our shit-eating grins
for the ticket seller behind bars who didn't give a shit
for our shit, just wanted bribes for good seats.
Somewhere in the city, Iggy Pop tried out lyrics
to "I Wanna Be Your Dog" and somewhere
Aretha cleared her throat and the MC Five
turned it up another notch. After the game, we waited
on the wrong side of the street for the bus home
as the sun vamoosed, Billy Bowen clutching the two-ton ham
he won in the lucky number scorebook drawing.
Some young Black men joined us, and Billy just
handed over the ham because our pastor
had been mugged outside the stadium last year,
but one guy said *Keep your damn ham, white boy*!
and we got on a bus that only took us further from home.
Denny McLain's in jail for the second time—raiding
the pension fund of his own company. Denny drank
a case of Pepsi every day. He had one more good season,
then spontaneously combusted. Like Detroit in '67. One match,
and nobody to blow out the candle. When his brother Paul
pitched a no-hitter in game two of a doubleheader
back in the '30s, Dizzy said, *If I'd a knowed Paul*
was gonna throw a no-hitter I woulda throwed one too—
I mean Dizzy Gillepsie. But all I know about jazz
could fit into one of Dizzy's cheeks. Those cheeks

were the size of grapefruit, but still. If I'd a knowed.
Dizzy Dean, Southern boy. Before Jackie Robinson landed
and his spikes caught in the dirt, and held.
I always drank my liquor straight and paid the price for it
directly. I haven't had a shot in eighteen years, and even that,
a reluctant toast. I can't pretend to like jazz. Iggy's music
mixed in the pounding din of car factories. We are all Stooges.
I wanna be your dog. Your frog. Your fog. Your warthog.
No one will ever win 30 games again, and so what?
Is the ham still riding around Detroit on a slashed bus seat
duct-tape silver over green vinyl? Nah.
James Brown repeats "I" nine times in a row
on "Please, Please, Please." "Riot," was an easy word to make
from "Detroit" for those who thought it was a game. It was
all about how you articulated "I" in 1967. In 1968. In 1979,
the singer Eddie Jefferson gunned down "gangland style"
outside Baker's Keyboard Lounge, *the* place to hear jazz in
   Detroit.
If I'da knowed, I'da throwed. I'm back in line at the turnstile,
2008. Outside the abandoned stadium. *But they built*
a new one! They built a new one! everybody says
like that's "some kind of wonderful." And don't get me started
on casino gambling. Dizzy. Miles/Bird/Trane. Am I validated
   now?
Am I authentic? Do I get to keep the ham? The autographed ball?
The free tickets to the next inappropriate comment?
I didn't live in Detroit. I lived in Warren. My Molotov
cocktail was a dud, but I went to jail for it anyway.
It's hard to punch yourself hard as hard as Adam Jenson did
in 1978 when he had that bad acid trip
and guzzling a fifth of whiskey wouldn't knock
him out. He didn't die! Exclamation point!
I'm going to change my name to Billy Ocean.
I'm going to get tough and get going.
I used to count things obsessively, but I stopped.
Somewhere a car door slams. It's the sound

of a drum set crashing. I want to like jazz!
But I don't! We all got our ways of spitting
out the chaos. I'm going to change my name
to Jayandee and get arrested for rapping backward
and upside down and crossing Eight Mile into Detroit
in my Emperor's Clothes. I'm buried in
nostalgia for Little Stevie Wonder. Blinded by the light
of his pure joy. I want to be Little Jimmy Daniels.
A little shame goes a long way to stir the drink.
So when Black Willie Horton scored
the winning run and Denny McLain hugged him,
we could believe for 3.4 seconds that the city wasn't
going to burn down again. The underground salt mines
of fiery tears distilled. We were speed not heroin.
We stood destroying our hearing and refused to dance.
Thus, I conclude. Thus, I make the sign of the cross
even though I don't believe: *Miles, Trane, Bird, Dizzy.*

Rowing Through the Ashes

The Buddhist monk Thich Quang Duc . . . at a downtown crossroads in Saigon sat in the lotus posture and, in a state of meditative control, burned himself to death in protest.

In Vietnam, we rowed an old wooden boat
down and around the lush green our country
tried to destroy, stopping to visit temples
and admire simple gifts of orange things:

food and flowers, boxes of crackers,
wrinkled bills. No one touches
the offerings. The world is in no hurry
here. I didn't understand Vietnam

as a boy and understand even less
as a man. Is complexity quicksand,
or is that simplicity? The more I learned
about Vietnam, the more shame I felt.

When a young boy on shore smiled
and gave me the finger, I just nodded.
No way to get lost on that long,
meandering lake. Do they teach

meandering in basic training? Old
enough to get a draft card, young
enough to miss getting called.
Lyndon Johnson on TV, *my fellow*

Americans. Our father let us change
the channel to the Canadian station
with Popeye cartoons, televised limbo
contests, and curling. Canada, close

enough to row to. Drive through a tunnel
beneath the river to. Friendly border.
They waved us through. Years later,
my parents admitted they would have

let me cross that river if I'd won
the death lottery. An old man on the train
from Hanoi held up his hand
to keep me from sitting beside him

then later let a woman take that seat.
He made room. No hard feelings.
They dug a lot of tunnels in Vietnam—
pretty cramped down there.

We forced them underground.
Or into caves. At Ninh Binh, we row
through many tunnels, ducking to avoid
low ceilings. I bumped my head once,

but not again. Lyndon Johnson seemed
so sad with his big ears and big nose.
My fellow Americans, shoveling
more teenagers over there to die.

Don't ask me why. Don't make me lie.
Maybe we should have left the news on
more often. The casualty numbers
always said we'd killed more of them

and thus were winning. No one I knew
had died yet. I was still living in the Canada
of grief. Limber enough to limbo lower.
Old enough to have friends who'd either

take the death leap or take their business
elsewhere or starve to fail their physicals
only to get called back and have to starve
all over again in order to be called one

of the lucky ones. Quiet on the water
just the paddles' light dive and curve
from morning into afternoon, until
we looped back through one final cave

where urns of monks' ashes sat stored
in crags on either side. Safe in that darkness
we bowed our heads to all we didn't
know, then to all we don't know now,

then to all we pretended not to know,
lost in time, despite knowing our location
in space, gliding through the urns of ashes
toward the light.

Google Maps: Street View, Warren

Fifteen years ago, I pulled my car to the curb
next to the manhole cover in front of our house
for the last time. For forty years, I'd deposited
small stones, big secrets, and my own spit
for good measure, down into those blind eyes.

I'm rounding off—everything else, recorded history.
From a rainy day thousands of miles away, I google
back those long gray cement slabs, the flat grid,
for a virtual walk around the block: rusted railing
my father installed, check. Pine tree stolen from
Up North, check. Creosoted streetlight pole, check.

I recite the names—dead or gone, down the block.
3-bedroom ranches from the smudged map
of the '50s. Driveway still rivered with my father's
tar streams when he tired of concrete crack filler
that never lasted through winter's fierce blasts.

Lawns half-brown, trees in leaf. Click. Click.
Bored already, fatigued by mirages of emotion
on what looks like one of world's dullest streets.
But still our anchors scraped as we drove
away to condos, senior living, cemeteries.

Close your eyes and imagine: young girls playing
cheerleader, few of them perky or peppy enough
to make the cut, or already smoking in the parking lot,
mocking the tryouts. Boys gathered on bikes, hooting
and—I've already forgotten the sounds we made,

the punctuation of curses. Nothing stopped the wind,
not parked cars or dead trees or sirens. But I know
who's left behind those closed doors where I might knock
and be recognized. Down to two: The Kloceks, garage
packed with junk to burden surviving children,

and Mr. Mazorak, so tiny and mean, no one's sure
he's still in there. Perhaps he's dug out and escaped
with what he believes are family secrets: bastard Ricky,
gay Roger, pregnant Renee. I'm worrying these houses
down to nubs, seeing them online, through the distorted

lens of the passing camera. Cloudy. They got that right.
Follow me as we turn the corner in front of the old
Ernst house onto Bach across from the old Keller place,
and you will see a young Black kid on a bicycle
too small for him. He wears a long white T-shirt,

black hoodie slung over one shoulder. He looks
straight at the camera. The only person visible
on the entire block. A Black kid where
no Black kids wandered, even lost.
I'm gone, so I can't tell what

he's in the middle of saying.
A slight blur in his features, but he looks
at home, casual smile in the bike seat
of someone who knows where he's going.

He doesn't know me from the impassive eyes
of the manhole cover, the anonymous camera
roving, robotic, leeching memory from cement.
Are you lost? he might be asking. *Can I help you?*

Homeless Suite

Across the street, a woman stops
at piled garbage in open plastic barrels
out for pickup, fishing in to pick out
three paper shopping bags, dumping
their contents back into the barrel
carefully refolding the bags, walking
away with them under her arm—
like she's arresting them / protecting
and cuddling them / like she's going
to store her dreams in them / I hope
they don't smell too bad. The dreams.

*

I'm not saying she's homeless or not.
Not for me to say. Today on the river trail,
I watched two men tie up tarps on their new
encampment, having been booted out
of the old encampment downtown yesterday.
The city made a show of helping them

dismantle, scribbling notes for the cameras
but at the end of the day most were left
to their own soiled devices. Some lay
in sleeping bags in the rain this morning.
Rain, the one thing we share. It's not for me
to say very much these days. I got a new
lock on my door yesterday, one of those
keyless electronic ones, and yet
I can't remove the old key from my ring.

*

The city is tiny-talking about building
tiny houses. Jesus is a write-in candidate
for mayor. Where do the homeless vote?
I'm asking for a friend. The new tents
go up beneath a bridge with all the joy-
less drudge of soldiers tired of battle.

I don't know much firsthand. Even less
secondhand. I need to put the electric
stim on my back to keep me from
spasming out on the floor. Or perhaps
simply to wake me up. Homelessness.
Two esses trailing off into a hiss.
Boo. Hiss. Homeless. Encampment.
One of the new guys says hello.
I give him a wave—the equivalent
of a slap across the face? See,
that's where they're at, in one long
present-tense saga. In the table

of contents, a series of asterisks
covers their faces when they talk.
Along the river last month
someone had let an unwanted
guinea pig loose. After spottings,
photos, online attestations,
the animal community lost its shit
trying to capture and save it.

To capture and save. To contract
or contradict. A neighbor walks
down the street picking up
garbage blown from trashcans.
I saw an exterminator emerge
from his house this morning
with his spray gun. The neighbor
held his child in his arms.
The boy was waving.

*

We've all got delete buttons now.
Things have been trickling down
like the dye from Ronald Reagan's
hair for over forty years and it still
hasn't reached them—the homeless
less. . . . That poor guinea pig.

We all can use a few paper grocery bags.
You can draw faces on them and cut out
holes for your eyes and mouth. Or
put groceries in them. I have no more
idea than the mayor. My own dreams
have a distinct odor, as if something
has turned. All I know is that we all
live in tiny houses. God help us.

If a poem is a house

and I think it is, are the windows
open or closed? If closed,
are they broken, air seeping in
cracks, tinkling through
broken glass? Are there curtains,
blinds, heavy wooden shutters?

I have the bricks, but not
the windows, not the doors.
How many doors does a poem have?
A front door, a side door,
back door, basement door?
Are they locked?

A question mark is a master key
but what if there's a deadbolt?
Are we outside the poem
or inside? Do we feel
claustrophobic or safe? How safe
is too safe? Germs on the door
handle? Graffiti on the walls?

Is the house infested
with vermin or roaches,
carpenter ants or carpenters?
If the house has a pet
does it come when called?
Is that a bat up in the attic
and are we okay with that?

If a poem is a house,
does the mail pile up on the floor?
Who knocks on the door?
Nobody robs the poetry house
and nobody makes donations.

It is just a house
where somebody lives
breath by breath.
See how the windows fog.

Gun-Shy

Gun-Shy, Warren, Michigan

FACT: The 40 oz is a hard-hitting, piss-yellow, oblong bottle of 5% abv malt liquor that gets warm before you even hit the bottom of the glass.
FACT: It embodies every aspect of American life: cheap pleasure without the hard work.
Hypothesis: The 40 is the most patriotic drink in America.

Nothing says America like an ice-cold can of mass-produced beer. Anheuser-Busch announced today that the company is replacing the Budweiser logo with "America" on its 12-oz cans and bottles this summer.

Gun-shy—I've always been more
than a little, even before I got one
shoved in my face up close and personal

behind a liquor store cash register
in Warren on the Detroit border.
Age 16, I was working on getting laid,
shy until drunk, then subtle as a gun.

*

When Roy Tubbs down the street still went
to school, sometimes we shared a joint
on the way—a smile-and-a-joke kind of guy,
that early, and stoned.

After he shot his father, I wanted to ask him
why, but never saw him again, though his father
returned to fertilizing lawns with his red truck—

not shy about missing three fingers
on the hand he'd raised against dying.

*

The first two shootings I knew
were both in-family, both on our block.
The other one, in a family with my last name,

lived across the street from Tubbs
and two doors down.

On a snow day from school, a kid shot
his little sister, no one to call timeout
to referee or even shovel.

The ambulance spun out, got stuck.
We emerged to pelt it with snowballs
like we did to cop cars, though,
once better informed, we pushed it out of ruts.

*

School figures in this too, as in, at least
graduate before you ruin your life.
But Patience was not the name
of any of our gangs or drugs
or sports teams.

Unrelated to the Black guys with guns
on their shopping trip for cash,
I was not shot in the store that day.
I mention Black because we were all
white on our block, indiscriminate
with grudges and guns.

*

My distant lunar cousin
on a field trip from Detroit for cash
left a can of Colt .45 on the counter—
a jokester side of him he did not reveal
while waving his gun and raising his voice

in an impolite way. The can sweat
a wet circle onto the counter.
Colt's horseshoe logo, and a bucking

bronco to suggest the alcoholic kick
of malt liquor, high on the arms list.

Their slogan *it works every time*
is subject to a range of interpretation
of the approximate size of a bullet hole.
Solve referent for *it*.

The Houston Colt .45s baseball team
sported a large gun on their uniforms
till they became the Astros and moved
indoors to get out of the heat. Thus,
the great invention of plastic grass.
I salute them with a can of America.

*

The Washington Bullets are gone,
but not the Houston Rockets. No sign
of the Hand Grenades, Bazookas,
or Nuclear Bombs, but the Axe Murderers
have a long tradition on their side.

The police arrived from the white side
of 8 Mile and spat slurs at the scene, loitering
in the ancient air-conditioning racket
of that tiny store crammed with liquor.
They told us they would not solve the crime
due to our proximity to 8 Mile and their
inability to tell one Black man from another.

Alive, and inordinately proud I had not
peed my pants, I mentally embellished
the story to tell my girlfriend Paula after work
with whom *it* was almost *working*.
My boss was inordinately proud of me
for not caving in and handing

over the twenties and checks hidden
in an empty cigarette carton.

I'm looking for another place to use
inordinately. Perhaps Mr. Tubbs
was inordinately proud that his son
had not killed him. Roy had good dope
but moved on to better dope
that made him a little edgy when
Mother Hubbard's cupboard was bare.

His mother was hidden in an empty
cigarette carton somewhere. How
Mr. Tubbs got custody was beyond
the toxic limits of our lawn-fertilized
imaginations. We had an affinity for poison,
where Patience was not a brand of condoms,
much less a virtue. Virtue was a cigarette brand.
Menthol or regular, filtered or unfiltered, though
Marlboro hard-luck pack was our big seller.

I don't own a gun, but I'm related
to white people who do. Police cars
have cameras now. Warren cops haven't
killed any unarmed Black men.
As far as I know. My wallet
is full of qualifications.

*

Matches were free. I checked IDs,
though not legal myself. I dreamed
of my name in neon, not on wanted posters,
but we never told each other our dreams,
so it didn't much matter either way.
Colt .45 tasted like shit, even when guzzled
out of quart bottles. My favorite combo:

a quart of Colt and a bottle of Ripple wine.
A kind of surf and turf or barf and scarf
for the sophisticated teenage set
inordinately fond of puking

then moving on. No big deal—
just the service charge for the buzz.
I never guzzled Colt .45 again
after the robbery. They recovered
no fingerprints, and I recovered
my bravado with Paula
who smoked True Blues

and knew a special occasion
when it hit us over the head
with a gun handle so we culminated
our relationship that night
in the damp grass of her parents' yard
behind the blow-up kiddy pool
using a condom handed down
by my older brother—the traditional
Trojan, which was better than
pulling out, a reckless maneuver
that did not work with her next
boyfriend Laffy Stinkbomb.

His first name *was* Laffy.
Stinkbomb, just a term of affection.
Their kid could be at least 40 by now.
I don't think they named him Laffy Junior.
I was happy Laffy Senior did not have
a gun, given his jealous nature.

It's like politics, I tried to explain one day
as he choked me against my locker
after auto shop. On the other hand,

Danny Krause, who I pinned in 15 seconds
in the gym class wrestling tournament, had
a gun, and went on to shoot a business associate
in a start-up drug operation and dump his body
in a snow bank at the junior high.

I could still put someone in a cross-face cradle
if circumstances warranted, though I suspect
if Danny is out of prison and looking for me
he wouldn't wait for the sadistic gym teacher
to blow the whistle. Sadistic gym teachers
were a dime a dozen back then, which must
make them a dollar a dozen, given inflation
and more sophisticated recreational facilities.

I had a chance to buy a handgun
out of the trunk of Matt Schmitt's LTD
in the parking lot by the abandoned tennis
court behind Shaw Parklet, but it was like
with the prostitutes we gave a jump to
outside the Top Hat at 3 a.m. one Christmas Eve,
who, given the holiday spirit, offered to go
down on us for free.

Both Matt and the hookers were cheerful
enough about my cowardice, or,
as I call it now, my judiciousness.
I had this crazy idea being a Daniels
on Rome Street meant I should have a gun
in case somebody mistook me for the other guy
whose name, no shit, was Tim, just one letter off.

My whole life, I've been one letter off, for better,
for worse. You might be able to take it out
before you come, but once you pull the trigger,

there's no reverse. And if I sound particularly full
of shit, just remember *it works every time.*

Over forty years ago, on the spot
where that store still stands, I followed
the firefly of a gun waving through the store
in a mad hysterical panic while the kid—not
much older than me—used an inordinate number
of variations on the word *fuck*, given
the brevity of our conversation. If *fuck*

is the bullet of words, I'll take the word
itself every time. Chaldeans own the store
now—Christian Arabs, a concept a lot
of those who drink America don't quite get.
I admire the computerized cash register
and bulletproof revolving counter. 99%
of Detroit party stores are owned by Chaldeans.
The other 1% by members of the Patience MC.

*

When we were kids—me and Laffy
and the rest—the Canadian TV station
out of Windsor broadcast limbo contests
right after Popeye each weekday night.
In Canada, they set the bar lower,
since a gun would just get in the way
of doing the limbo, while in Detroit,
the wobbly bar for peace and justice
was as low as it could go, and people
still tripped over it.

*

Despite slander to the contrary, we were
pretty good at shooting each other up back

in the old neighborhood after the '67 uprising
when we got guns to protect us from imaginary
gangs of Black kids gathering on the other side
of 8 Mile. We were stupid enough
to believe we had something they wanted
while we worked at the same factories
made the same money and drove the same
damn cars we all helped build.

It didn't take much to make me gun-shy
for life, but that doesn't mean we shouldn't
have had a meet-up down on 8 Mile
where some people with charts and not a whole lot
of patience drew lines on maps that went far afield
from 8 Mile with a bunch of X's to show us
where all the money was really buried
so that if we could all agree on taking turns shoveling,
we might dig up something somewhere to share.

*

Is giving a jump to a couple stranded hookers
in the Top Hat parking lot the best thing I ever did?
Or, wait, are they the ones who gave us a jump?

Roy Tubbs and his father never seemed shy
to me. In daylight, always ready to give you
a smile beneath their sunglasses,
as if you knew something and they knew
something and the rest of the world beyond
Rome Street didn't have a clue.

*

One sober afternoon, Marlene,
Roy's younger sister, invited me in
to their dark empty house. I wasn't sure
I was going to mention Marlene at all—

hers was my first funeral and she, my first kiss—
it seems like too much for this story packed
with lies, overlapping with lies, like the narrow
brick houses on our narrower streets.
Marlene showed me her father's guns
and offered me lemonade, homemade
with one of those frozen cans you emptied
out and added a can of water to.

We made up a lot of our own definitions
and nicknames, bored with lighting up
those free packs of matches and tossing them
in the street where they burned out. If the guy
had shot me for not giving up our hiding place,
I wouldn't have gotten laid that night
though maybe someone would have lit
a candle for me in church before heading out
to the parking lot to light up a Truth.

I can't remember everything
but I do not have to, being white.

*

If we'd had a meet-up on 8 Mile
maybe I would've run into my Black relative
adopted specifically for this poem
and he could have told me what
a patronizing motherfucker I was,
and we could have shaken hands
and said, *Hard feelings*, and been honest
on that unforgiving road.

*

Growing up, we had no protection
from guns or story problems.
The math nearly killed us all.

Being white, I can joke about it:
sex and guns. The other Daniels
shooting his sister. They did not
catch the robber with the gun.
He's probably out there wearing
a throw-back Colt .45 jersey
for old-timers night.

The kid shouted at me
where's your fucking hiding place
because all white people
have hiding places, even while making
less than minimum wage at a corner store
on the edge of Detroit. It's a luxury,
and he was out to collect luxury tax.

I still burned with hot-sweat anger and fear.
That's the way it's supposed to work, hating
on each other over nickels and dimes
when we're all in the same damn zip code,
area code, the same class, the same teachers
flunking us on exams for Patience and Virtue.
The rust on our automobiles
the same color. I have no authority,
having stabbed myself
with my fake badge. Fake guns
aren't so fake anymore.

*

For much of my life
I've resisted parking
between the yellow lines,
but not all of my life,

my life, my life. Sixty
years, and I've never

felt like I might be shot
again. At sixty,
still allowed to be shy
in all this white space.

House of Drumming, House of Song

House of Drumming, House of Song

Here in Pittsburgh, my teenage son and daughter
sing their carefree, fizzy joy. Digging
in the yard, I hear their voices
rise and fall through open windows.
They can carry a tune. They have pockets
big enough, sewn by minor gods
with magic thread and endless dreaming.

In Detroit, we never sang.
Not the boys, not the girls.
We listened to rock so loud our ears
smoked, but we were not singers.
We drummed car seats, dashboards,
and each other. We lit lighters
and held them aloft at arena shows.

How could singing be for sissies
when our heroes sang? Equations
and formulas, mysteries and historical texts,
electrical currents and gym class ordeals,
red arrows and one-way streets, woofers
and tweeters and teeters and totters
all led to the same factory boats,
both anchored and beached on the shore
of the Lake of Industry where we would row
in sand to the gritty stop of retirement,
bailing water the whole time, mechanizing even
our dreams, cutting them short with precision tools
so that breathing itself became our only song.

We lost the hook. Never found the refrain.
We played extended drum solos identical
to our fathers' while the crowd slipped away
to the john, or made out, or passed joints,
or simply nodded off, while the rest of the band
drifted into shadows of dazed drinking.

When they returned, we accepted polite applause
for our endurance and steadfast lack of creativity.

My father never sang. In the middle of sweeping,
my mother sometimes burst into song, grabbing
the closest child and howling—Ozzy Osbourne
combined with Patsy Cline at warp speed.
She seemed so happily out of herself
that we fled. Laughing, she chased us.
We laughed too, afraid of wanting
to be caught.

I continue to not sing except alone
in fast-moving automobiles, though I left
that old life long ago, the heavy-metal job,
the muffled solitary drumming,
long lines of tiny bodies, somebody smirking
that we all look alike from above.

I dropped through the trap door
and into what I've been calling my life
for the last thirty years. If there's a beat
of a different drum, I have not heard it.

I want to carry one long note
that slowly sinks into silence.
My family jokes that our "Happy Birthday"
gets the dogs a-howling, so we avoid
even that—straight to cake and ice cream.
We vote for listening, we vote
for mad clapping. We vote for golden
oldies. We endorse the air guitar
and the broomstick mike of lip synching.

My mother hobbled by daily pain—
I have not heard her sing

in two thousand years. Math
and song were entirely outside
the singed circle of our existence.

My mother, a red planet
on her own rectangular urban orbit.
I want to hear her say, *You don't like*
my singing? I'll just sing louder
and longer. A lesson we should
have learned: to hell with polite applause.

Even the weeds enjoy getting pulled,
or so I imagine, freed by the dazzle and flash
and sheer volume of my children's young voices,
the sound waves on their way to Mars or Cincinnati
or to the apartment in Sterling Heights, Michigan,

where my 85-year-old parents are just now stirring,
and perhaps while my father makes coffee
and my blind mother attempts to butter toast,
not her fingers, somebody, against
all odds, might briefly
and quietly
hum.

Soft Side of the Moon

City-heat concrete. No mercy or memory.
No give. Take. Night simmers fear, stirs.

Results offer no surprises:
Body count. Shrug. Aftertaste. Cringe

outstays its welcome. Trust lands belly-up
on the curb. Ask the mayor if he knows

where your street is and why they never pave it,
why they just patch the potholes one more time

and get the hell out of there. Hell that cannot be
patched over, blended or mended.

Apostrophes of sweat. Inconsiderate sighs
hot in your face. Face to face over drugs

to spiral up and out. The mayor
has free tickets. Good seats. The mayor

is gelling his hair and covering his ass.
The moon nostalgic for mis-

directed prayers and sincere propositions,
tired of the odd bargaining of the damned.

City-heat concrete puts your life in parentheses,
your smile in a life jacket, your head in the yoke

of straight-ahead-no-eye-contact. You have
a few things to say to the mayor

but he's established a hotline
to fry your phone calls. City council

sues each other over who has to pay
whose lawyers.

Talk radio has all the answers.
Even the moon is booing.

City-heat concrete. August taking
an illegal extension on the back end,

off the books. The Fan Man recites
rhyming couplets while AC salesmen

scat in their ice-powered suits.
Listen tonight to who backs down

and who simply goes down
and who simply stays down

and who rises again. City fault lines
go unpaved, unexamined, glued over

with spit and bribes.
The guy with the knife is just lonely.

The guy with the gun is just having
a bad day with Despair and their children.

And you, you're waiting for it to cool down.
You've got a hard-on for the moon

and a running battle with the dollar bill.
If only the police would stop by tonight

to brush your hair and pat you on the ass,
maybe you could visit your old friend Sleep,

living in a cool basement somewhere
on the other side of the moon.

If You Ever Have to Do This Yourself

My daughter started crying
when she couldn't get the fake poop back
into the fake butt of the Pooping Dog
she won at the school carnival. She'd squeezed
too hard, and the poop popped out
in the car on the way home. We'd eaten
half-frozen fries and gristly hot dogs.
All for a good cause.

She's in first grade. My son's in third.
His dog still has its poop. She doesn't want me
to say *potty* anymore—too babyish—
yet she was bawling. I lost it, shouting
to scare us all. Back home, I got them
into bed, my daughter still snuffling, my son
glazed over into silence.

Shamed, I stood in the kitchen jamming
the orange rubber cylinder of poop
back up the plastic dog's butt.
I used index finger, I used thumb,
I used tack hammer. I wet the poop,
then squeezed with needle-nose pliers

until I got it all back in.
Two Pooping Dogs on the counter
for them to find in the morning.
To write their names on in Sharpie.

They kissed me when I awoke.
They held their puppies. We have no pets,
though they're always asking.
If you ever have to do this yourself,
keep it together. Shut up
and do love's dirty work.

Dim

Today my son realized someone's smarter
than him. Not me or his mom—
he still thinks we know everything.
One of the other kids, Nathan, made fun
of him at the computer for screwing up
at the math game. Other kids laughed.
2nd grade. *I'm never gonna be as smart*
as him, he says.
                                        I'm never gonna be smart
as half my students if we're talking IQs.
He doesn't want me to explain.
He wants me to acknowledge
that he's dumb. He's lying in bed,
taking his glasses off and on,
trying to get them perfectly clean
for the morning. I'm looking around
his dark room for a joke or some
decent words to lay on him. His eyes
glassy with almost-tears.
The world wants to call on him.
I take his hand in mine.

Fishing in the Cement Pond

Schenley Park, Pittsburgh

Most people don't even know about the pond
at the bottom of the deep hollow, reached
only by an ancient staircase crumbling down
the hillside. We slid down on our asses
with our plastic poles and can of worms dug
from our yard's hard dirt. My son, six,
the pond enormous in his squint.

Under the shadow of the high bridge, among
crushed appliances and bald tires, green glass shards
and disintegrating cardboard, we sat on the pond's
cement lip—man-made and man-ruined,
yet fat, wizened catfish, murky shadows of carp,
wallowed. Flimsy bluegill shimmered with illusion.
He wanted to keep his first. It swallowed the hook.

I wiggled it out, returned the fish to water,
but it floated back toward us through the murk.
We could almost see our house above the hillside
but my son was glad we couldn't. We saw a large man
on a milk crate fishing as if he cared. My son wanted to row
across on a raft of tires or in a fridge with the door removed.

Above us, the city passed another hot, endless August day.
Traffic from the freeway hissed through trees.
Our dead fish shone flat in the sun. The blind fisherman
flinched at our casting. He asked my son to tell him
what he saw, and was told a tale of gigantic proportions.
The man cocked his head and laughed. *I do believe*
I hear the waves, he said. The cement pond—
giant seashell or rusted car—magnified all sound.

We ran out of worms or the fish stopped biting.
A thin line of sweat glistened on my son's upper lip.
He'd caught his first fish and talked to a blind man.
The city waited above us with red signs and yellow lines.
Can we get lost on the way home? he asked. *You need*
a map for that, I said. We struggled up the broken steps.
How did the blind man get down there? he asked.
The sea was vast and unknowable.

Defeat in the City Game

We stood waiting for the school bus
while three men argued over a stolen
cell phone. Me, my son, my daughter.
7:53. Where was the damn bus?
The big guy jiggling his hammy fist
vs. the little guy with baggy pants,
the ragged splinter of a junkie wedged
between them. Baggy pants, hand
in his pocket, claimed he had a gun,
gonna blow the hammy head
off. We're just this cute little family
of statues in the line of fire. Hammy
charged off around the corner,
the bus came, my children climbed on,
the other men vanished.

And there it is. Elusive It, fugitive It.
Scary It. Irrational—or just practical—It.
Back home with my spreadsheet
of potential actions I could/should
have taken, I slashed around
what/whether to tell my wife,
what my children were actually
aware of. I promised to stop using
the word *actually* so much.
It's losing meaning in terms
of what was in baggy's pocket
though he claimed it was
loaded. Next day, I told the driver
we're waiting across the street
from now on.

As the last seconds ticked off
and my children's hands turned to ice,
as the crowd filed out of the arena,
as the clouds drifted by unnoticed.
It. 7:53. The zeroes
of my children's eyes
narrowing.

Punching the Numbers

Two old men at the lottery/check-cashing
window grip aluminum canes and wait,
their lucky numbers memorized,
to be rattled off confidently in turn.
Straight. Boxed. Daily. Big Four.
Super Seven. The clerk will punch them
in just as quickly, the chain of her glasses
dangling, swaying, metronome
of dollar dreams, clutching the elusive.
One cane three-pronged, one rubber-tipped.

At the window, a young man speaks
a steady sweaty stream. The computer
says he's already cashed two checks today
each at a different store. *What kinda check
you cashing?* The clerk steams bulletproof
between them. His hands wobble
and twist on the slim counter. *Boy needs
a cane himself*, one man says.
The computer says . . . she says.

You don't need it, she says.
Whatever it is, you don't.
The line sways back,
gives him space. *Go home.*
The clerk pushed a flat hand
against the smudged glass.
Her glasses and chain taut
against her chest. She calls security
on the tinny intercom. *You don't
need. . . .* His skin sizzles
with fake love and high damage.
He raises both arms, *Fuck you,
all of you*, the bad check flaps
in one hand as he backs toward

the door. As if he's just committed
a robbery. But already

one cane hooks the counter, the line
pulled tight again with the willingness
to give it up. 531, 470, 8863, 25, 36, 17,
the chanting of the old monks begins.

Outrage at the Laundromat

One stray dog trots in the open door
and on top of a basket of clean clothes
with its caked muddy paws, then under
the flat folding tables. An enormous
young woman stripped down to her bra
in the wild summer heat chases it out the door.
The rest of us, sweating, resigned to the spin
cycle, do not budge. She's screaming,
I'll kill that fucking dog, as she storms back
in. Maybe somebody's smirk sets her
off. She turns on us. *Do I look like I got*
any more fucking quarters? Her skin
a beautiful sheen of sweat. Okay.
We slap them down on the table
in front of her until she has enough
to start over.

Last night I drove my son home

from his friend's house, where they were filming
a movie starring my son in a love triangle—
fifteen, he's never been in a love right angle,
or even a love straight line, as far as I know.
He stopped talking two years ago—to me, I mean.
I got this secondhand from a street informant
I'll refer to by her code name, Little Sister.

Warm night, windows rolled down—
my cheap car requires physical cranking.
(Not even a CD player!) Purchased back when
he was ten and still kissed me goodnight
and may even have held my hand
as we watched old movies. (No cable TV!)
Yesterday he made me kill a giant bug
and I briefly saw that ten-year-old again.

Full moon—I saw him look up, following
it as I turned and we lost it to the trees.
September, but moist like August. In that silence
I ached for a few soft words between us.

On a sidewalk near the park a young man sat,
face in hands. A friend stood helpless above him.
I slowed down. *What's that guy doing?*
Is he OK? I said. *I see him too*, my son said.
The friend helped the man to his feet, and I drove on.

My son hummed an old song about the moon
I didn't know he knew. My son, the star
of a movie I'll never see. I just get
these vague coming attractions.
I caught him in a lie or two last week.
Every exchange a house of cards—all it takes
is a deep sigh, and they tumble down.

I'd have hummed along with him,
but I didn't want him to stop.

Private Room

My daughter got sick and nearly died—
fall of ninth grade. She combed her hair out.
I kissed her goodbye and goodnight

each time I left, and she had no choice,
attached to grim tubes, prone, ashen.
My daughter sick and nearly dying

of embarrassment as doctors probed
the mystery and fought among themselves.
I missed her goodbyes and goodnights.

We watched an old movie from child-
hood. No game shows or reality. Fourteen.
My daughter. Sick with worry she

would die, I slept on the floor and wept.
I pressed ice packs against her to stop tremors,
then kissed her, since I could. Goodnight

seemed insufficient. So did I. No curfew
in that moonless room without boys.
My daughter got sick. Death passed her by—
I snuck her home. We did not kiss. Goodnight.

Thankful for the Moon

Last night I dreamt my teenage daughter clung
to me with the desperate love of childhood.
Snow today. While my teenage son
sleeps off his mother's tantrum, I shovel.

My daughter's half-empty cereal bowl
sticks to the counter. We're in the stone age—
she's helping archeologists who'd never find
the dishwasher. Last night she retrieved

the stale marshmallows my wife had thrown
out, then gorged herself. I can't explain—
use your imagination. Last night I dreamt
my mother could still see.

She was laughing at a comic strip. She'd clip
and send me corny ones. She can't even see
this sweet snow angling down like—
my imagination fails me. My daughter

mocked our Grace last night.
She does not believe in God, she said,
so why say what she's thankful for,
and to who? *Us*, I should've said, *to us.*

I took away her dinner. We're not sure
about God ourselves, but look for something
positive in each day. That's corny. I'll take
corny. My wife made this great chili

with cornbread, but it was downhill
from there, a mudslide. Slogging through,
all of us covered in it. My son invented
a new face that made me want to smack him.

Too late to smack him, and I swore
I never would. He's bigger than me.
Raging accumulation in the just-cleared path
behind me. I'll have to re-shovel soon.

Or wake him up to help me.
I'm not up to that. He's not down with that.
I'm thankful I never hit him. About God,
I still wonder—as a child, I thought I knew.

Imagine someone inventing snow.
Be thankful, damn it. Yesterday,
while waiting to pick the kids up
from an after-school special

I watched the full moon. My car
idled in the parking lot. *Oh, moon*,
I said, and began to cry. My son
also thinks our Grace is stupid.

Sometimes it takes me forever
to think of something to say.
In lieu of God, I have the moon.
Our moon, though there are many others.

The Addict's Guide to Fatherhood

I placed a soft red rug at the bottom of the stairs to catch
my children when they fell. I clipped the commas
of their fingernails like an obsessed grammarian.
I collected the pebbles that *they'd* collected and discarded.
I discarded my own collections—empty bottles, needles.
I vacuumed up the dusty street I'd rode in on.
I clapped the erasers together, white dust offered up
to the god of pure intentions. Sun block and ipecac syrup.
Dream weavers and wind catchers. A kindly dentist
with a bubble machine and fairy assistants.
An old-school pediatrician with his home phone number.
Elmo Band-Aids and Scooby Doo Underoos and Beatrix Potter
everything else. Baby gates and universal child-proofing.
Glow-in-the-dark stars glued on
so the sky would not fall on them.

Heat of Departure

Ninety degrees of thick, rude heat—a summer guest
we can't get rid of—hovering over our city,

our brick house. Yet our son who's leaving home
tomorrow, we wish would stay. No AC in his room,

but a window unit in ours for wicked waves like this.
He's almost 18. *Can't sleep*, he says, and, though

we've offered before, now he quickly slips
his mattress on the floor in our room and plops

down. 6'5". His own room wrecked
with packing. His last three nights, a man

sprawled back into a boy before us. *The heat*,
we all keep saying, *it's awful*. In the morning

I rise early and turn off the AC
just to hear him breathing.

Gospel

I saw the great blue heron today,
still, above the flat horizon, staring
as I passed on my bike. Some mornings
I admit, I scare it into rising just to see
those wide whispering wings spread
over grape vines clenched into earth
in bright green rows. Nothing is here
for my amusement. The heron fishes
in the small stream where the narrow road
turns. Easy pickings. Today, I don't scare it.

My son dropped sticks off the narrow bridge
into that stream twenty years ago—a man now,
and I'm sad for it on days like this. Thousands
of miles away, he sings songs I've never heard.
Look, I'd say to him, and point. He's not here
for my amusement, getting on with it, screwing up,
muddling through. We used to watch current carry
those twigs till they disappeared. Sometimes
it's so quiet, I can hear wings. The heron, straight
graceful pin above flatlands along the stream.

To dig our roots deeper, or to fly? How to hide
nests, protect our young? My son is tall some-
where out there. We build nests one thin stick
at a time. The sticks never disappear. I don't
want to live far from water. My amusement
is finite. Leaves on the vines redden
and wither while elsewhere fruit ferments
into wine. It's an old story, I know,
but teach me the words, my son.

Witnesses

I was painting the hall and stairway
"River Mist" when Witnesses knocked
at the door looking so sincere I wanted
to pelt them with water balloons.

The dog next door already barking.
I said, *I don't have cable.* They said,
That's why we're here. I raised River Mist
hands over my face in a protective stance

familiar to monster movie aficionados.
It never saves anyone, and they weren't
going to save me. I was drowning
in the misty river. Next door, my neighbor

was photographing his own crumbling house—
for posterity? *Go away*! I shouted.
Someone wanted to steal a small portion
of my soul. *I need that soul!*

The cable guy was tougher: *everyone on your street*
has cable, he said. *What's wrong with you?*
I don't believe! I cried. *In cable!* They both left
pamphlets in my mail slot claiming my damnation.

One channel versus 99. River Mist vs.
The Man in the Moon. The selling of souls
at an introductory rate. No one else ever
knocks on my door. Where have all the other

salesmen gone? Perhaps my neighbor has them locked
in his basement. They skip his house completely—
monster weeds, peeling paint, collapsing porch—
disconnected satellite dish picking up unholy signals.

River Mist. Blood on my hands. River missed. God's will.
If I had cable, I could get the Monster Movie Channel.
It's the paint. It's the ladder. It's the total coverage.
Why are they really here? What constitutes

a sale? A good day? Who cooks the books
for Jesus? How does anyone dress for success?
I wear my holey jeans. Paint blurs my knees.
If I knelt to pray, there'd be evidence.

Hard Crust

Cancer, she said, *I've got fucking cancer.*
She dropped the phone, then dropped
into mad tears, flung tears, bullet tears.
I held her, swallowing my own.

We were stuck drowning
in a conference center out of town.
Twin beds, shadowy angled ceiling
suddenly compressing our lives.

C for Cancer. D for Death.
All other letters obliterated. We squeezed
onto one bed. The tumor bullied itself
between us. If we ate, would we be feeding it?

We wanted to rush to a hospital, have someone
cut it out. Schedule surgery within the next
five seconds. The room smelled like AC
and the sterile grief of anticipation. If only—

the sentence unfinished due to the unfinished
sentence. That sharp C cut into her clenched fist.
I rose to pick up her phone before we stepped on it.
Though I wanted to. We'd have to make

our own calls soon, say the word aloud, over
and over, lacking detail, explanation, running
out of even tears. We were expected at a potluck.
Still four more days of conference—

no appointment to escape to, so we stayed.
With cancer, you can be anywhere. It follows you
into dark, intimate places and shopping malls.
They caught it early. She is still with me.

With us. Remember the smell of pure panic
released, the evil genie leaving the bottle
for good? Remember trying to eat some tough
and tasteless thing, chewing and chewing,

the C caught in the craw as you gulped
and swallowed? I gave her regrets at the potluck.
Under the weather. Just a touch of cancer,
I didn't say. I forgot to bring our covered dish.

Summer—many pies, but few main dishes.
I watched my watch, then took my leave.
Take some for her, the host said, sawing off
a slice, shoveling it onto a plate so that

I had no choice. Store bought, not homemade.
Even the rain on the walk back to her
did not soften it.

Talking About the Day

Each night after reading three books to my two children—
we each picked one—to unwind them into dreamland,
I'd turn off the light and sit between their beds
in the wide junkshop rocker I'd reupholstered blue,
still feeling the close-reading warmth of their bodies beside me,
and ask them to talk about the day—*we did this,*
we did that, sometimes leading somewhere, sometimes
not, but always ending up at the happy ending of *now.*
Now, in still darkness, listening to their breath slow and ease
into sleep's regular rhythm.
                                        Grown now, you might've guessed.
The past tense solid, unyielding, against the dropped bombs
of recent years. But how it calmed us then, rewinding
the gentle loop, and in the trusting darkness, pressing play.

American Cheese

Hot Dog Variations

I stuck potato sticks into my bun
and called it a porky pine.
They scraped my palette into bleeding.
My mother wrapped dogs in bacon
slit the side for a sliver of pickle
and called them gourmet.

A two-for-one coupon from Uni-mart.
They circled black on a spit under a pale bulb
and came back up on the swings in the park.
3 a.m., and we wanted to have sex again.
Downstairs, I boiled the dogs. We wrapped
them in white bread. We nearly choked.

I ate them cold from the package
rehearsing my speech about purity
on long-distance drug deliveries for Mad Mike.
God save the Hot Dog. Its wobble,
its cushioned fall into the bun. God bless
American condiments and baked beans.

It fell in the dirt, but I wiped it on my jeans.
It fell in the coals, but I wiped it on my jeans.
It fell off the platter, and I fought the dog for it.
I fought the dog and the dog won.
Relish and love. Madness and mustard.
Don't choke. Don't wince when you bite

into something hard. Grind it up and don't
grumble, don't mumble. Lord, it comes spilling
out the side, chili and onions and regret.
Wipe the corner of your mouth.
Grin like a good American. Grin
and don't hit anyone. Grin and load up

the grill. Grin and click the tongs
like a hungry gator. Cheap paper plates
sticking together like pure love.
Eat with your hands, in a hurry,
eat when you're poor, when
you don't give a shit—you just want
to gulp it down, get back to it.

American Cheese

At department parties, I eat cheeses
my parents never heard of—gooey
pale cheeses speaking garbled tongues.
I have acquired a taste, yes, and that's
okay, I tell myself. I grew up in a house
shaded by factory clank and clamor.
A house built like a square of sixty-four
American Singles, the ones my mother
made lunches with—for the hungry man
who disappeared into that factory
and five hungry kids. American Singles.
Yellow mustard. Day-old Wonder bread.
Not even Swiss, with its mysterious
holes. We were sparrows and starlings
still learning how the blue jay stole our eggs,
our nest eggs. 64 singles wrapped
in wax—dig your nails in to separate them.

When I come home, I crave—more than any
home cooking—those thin slices in the fridge.
I fold one in half, drop it in my mouth.
My mother can't understand. Doesn't remember
me being a cheese eater, plain like that.

Ode to the Reel Mower

When you stop pushing
it stops exactly *there*
absorbing the grace
of cut-grass silence.

*

It always starts. It never runs
out of gas. It does not
shoot your eye out
with a rock or glass shard.

*

It runs on dew and pollen
and sweat. It has never
woken one sleeping person.
It is never new and improved.

*

Grass falls gentle
onto itself like pages
of a favorite book.

*

If the blades need sharpening
a 150-year-old man with a large stone
in a damp basement will send up
faint sparks, accept no payment.

*

At night it trims
the moon's beard.

On Tears

Tears do not add up with the same firmness
of American quarters. Or dimes. Or pennies. They fall
with the urgency of escapees, no way to lose the dogs of grief
who will lick them up, swallow, and stand firm, panting, waiting
for more. Even Alice's pool of giant tears only measures
four inches deep. What if we all met in mourning and shed our
tears
into a large hole and created a new Great Salt Lake? Well,
if the moon were a wafer of bread, and the salty pond
the broth of redemption, we might have something.
But, there's no saving the moon. Somebody nibbling it
away every month. Or maybe the sky itself is the pool of tears
and the stars grains of salt. Or okra in the soup.
Tears fall and evaporate so quickly nobody has time
to lick or collect them, label and study them under microscopes
for self-pity or self-righteousness. Even the drip from the faucet
is bigger than one tear. Is there anything sadder than a tear
emerging
to weave down the landscape of the cheek, or even
down the neck? If they don't fly off the chin.
If you don't have somebody with a tissue saying *there there.*
Once you reach a certain age, nobody says *there there*
ever again. Maybe that's sadder. The last *there.*
And you're on your own, spilling them into small droplets
on the floor or the rug or the cement or the car seat
or the gravestone. And you're swallowing hard
and they count for nothing.

Firing the Late Person

I swing the back door open, and it tears a hole
in the green canvas awning sagging with snow.
Two mourning doves on the black wire briefly flutter
then land again, never straying far. We didn't use
the feeder this winter. Last fall, we cut down
the dead crab apple tree we'd hung it in.
I walk to a meeting where I will vote
on firing somebody. He will have trouble
finding another job. I shook the snow off
the awning and onto the ground. Too late
for the awning. What's he doing this morning?
Stroking his little white dog and killing himself
with mounds of snacks, knowing what's
coming? Their nest sits in the big pine tree
across the street—the illusion of a simple life.
We've already consulted a lawyer. He has too,
if he's smart. Is he the scraggly robin
that never flew south? My children in snow pants
and boots have waddled onto the school bus.
The tree stump's buried by snow, but we know
it's there. We assume the birds will survive without us
this winter, though some will surely die, like all birds
and people. His dog, just part of the problem,
one variant of his daily late arrival. I complicate
the fresh snow with footprints. The pine tree shivers
down a dusting that melts against my face.
I'm thinking about the awning.
What will it cost to fix, eh, lovebirds?

The Land of 3000 Dreams

They say if you just strap weights
around your ankles and wrists
and carry on
                    you will be stronger.
They say if you just attach weights
to your earlobes or genitalia
you will hear
                    your true love call your name.
They say if you just carry a coffin
above your head every day of your life
animals will love you
                              and you will accept death.
They say if you just wear a cast-iron hat
and tip it to your enemies
you will learn forgiveness
                                        or vengeance.
They say if you strap on a lead belt
and listen to Chubby Checker records
you will fuck
                    with dignity.
They say if you fill your mouth with gold
and chew raw meat like bubble gum
you will be both seen
                              and heard.
They say if you replace your hair
with steel rods and comb it
with a garden rake
                         it won't blow in the wind.
They say if you try to bench press a small automobile
you will be crushed.
                              They say there are limits
to what weights can do.
                                   They say the weight
of the heart plus the weight of the soul
cannot be lifted.
                         They say in the land of 3000 dreams

strong men and strong women
will have weak children
from being constantly lifted
from the weight of expectation
from the heavy words
raining down on them.

The Alone-Doors

Don't try this at home.
Try this on a wet dark road
with an unpromising destination—
hospital/funeral/prison—
or on just another useless errand
created by badly transcribed directions
for the good life
when all your calculations wash away
in the smear of steady rain
softly eroding the names of those you once
called *best friend* with all the sincerity
of a big-haired rock star on his first arena tour.

List the memories no one can confirm,
the alone-doors with the one key
spiked in your palm, burning off the acid
of nostalgia, tattooing the soft skin with loss
when all you want is to get it in the door
and turn and enter and witness again:

weeds behind the garage swaying tall
against the mesh fence like the long hair
of a girl you think you love
who will die with her braces on.
The neighbor's dog, belly swollen
with anonymous puppies, eyes softening
as you pet her pressed up against the fence.

The puppies disappear. The dog
disappears. You burn trash in a rusty barrel
and ash rises in the gray Detroit spring,
the last patch of snow in the angle of shade,
and the sundial of your young life
turns out to be a chalk drawing
by the deaf-mute down the block

who kicked your ass once—why?
Memories recede like the line of snow.

A rubber ball bounces against a wall
and returns, bounces, returns. A wounded
sparrow hops crooked near the curb
and you should find a way to put it out
of its misery. The ball bounces,
returns, the comfort of the wall
and its resistance, sky spiraling
into dusk, then night, and you're aiming
for the one brick, the perfect strike,
cheating for yourself, you alone
against brick, time, and a dying sparrow
waiting for a cat, watching you with a hard eye,
its silent intrusion into the rest of your life.

Punished, you bent over the furnace vent
in the floating dust of the silent house.
The others all at the fall festival
and its traveling carnival of greasy rides
and clumsy flirting. You, caught in a lie,
a twisted net of deceit your clumsy fingers
could not unravel, and all you have
is the furnace clicking on, and, hunched over,
you hog the heat, dismissing all other forms

of prayer. What did you lie about? Why
did he hit you? Who rode the Tilt-A-Whirl
with that girl? Hot breath whispered against
your face, into your hollow chest, your eyes
closed, listening. Are you still with me,
or are you nudging whoever's next to you,
tilting your head toward the exit?

The authority of the speaker has left
the building. I admit the deceit
of instructions leading nowhere
but to my alone-door where I will greet you
like the invisible friend you imagined
for two weeks during a bad stretch.

I have been practicing my coffee-stained
smile and my knee-worn patience
in front of the vacated jury of my peers
just for you. I have dreamt the world's
most comfortable chairs for us to sit in.
Listen, you will say. *Remember?* I'll say.

Can't Sleep

Two days after Eminem (Marshall Mathers) abruptly canceled his European tour, citing exhaustion and unspecified "other medical issues," his spokesperson revealed that the rapper has been hospitalized for a sleep-medication dependency. In response to news of Eminem's hospitalization, a radio station was collecting fan signatures on a 20-foot long "Get Well" card in Warren, Michigan. Warren is in Macomb County, the area where Eminem grew up.

Marshall Mathers and I cannot sleep
tonight. We lie in bed and remember Warren,
the same city of our separate youths, the perfect grid
from Eight Mile Road to Fourteen Mile Road.
From Dequindre to Hayes. He is 32.
I am 49. He is the illegitimate son of my memory.
I count the blocks, I list street names:
Dallas, Otis, Rome, Pearl, Jarvis, Garrick,
Michael, Toepfer. Then, the families
who lived in every house, and the children,
and which factory the fathers worked in,
who dropped out of high school
and who graduated. The names of the trailer
parks and places I got my ass kicked.
Where who got shot and who did the shooting.
Who got pregnant, who kept the baby. Who
didn't. But it's just six square miles,
and still I cannot sleep. If you drive
these streets, you might suddenly
and unknowingly end up in Sterling Heights
or Hazel Park, or, even Center Line,
but me and Marshall would know,
wouldn't we, Marshall? What are you
taking to get you out of the sleepless box
of Warren? I've got three bottles
in my medicine cabinet. Your mother could
have been any number of my classmates:
Lynn, Robin, Patty, Cindy, Judy. I already

took one pill, but I think I need half
of another one. Our neighbor is silent
tonight, though last night he was pounding
a sledgehammer at 4 a.m. so hard it shook
our house. We didn't try to stop him.
His phone is disconnected. Etc.
It's that etc. that we have in common.
Me and him—and you, Marshall.
He's alone next door now. His two children
from two wives ago rarely visit.
Here, my wife and two children,
we stay put. Tonight offers no sledge-
hammer of an excuse. If only the houses
had an upstairs. If only someone had thought
to create a downtown. If only the GM/Ford/Chrysler
plant had not closed down or laid off half
its workers. If only someone one time
had been less cruel. Had gotten off us, let us up
before blood was shed. I used to crave
drugs that kept me up: speed, coke.
The jerky knife-blades and shrieking volume
of rage. Tonight, the relentless silence
of the sledgehammer. The legalized
dancing monkey. Tonight it's Warren
on the brain, the dangling muffler
of what we thought we left behind.
Bullets in the bottles calling our names.

Shadow of a Doubt

The length of time it takes to swallow
a handful of pills is less than it takes
to hang yourself, shoot yourself,
slit your wrists, or jump off a bridge.
Based on hunch, assumption, rehearsal.
Depending on when you start the clock,
leap off the stolen motorcycle.
Given the lack of scientific evidence,
given anger and grief, an abundance
of blame, imagined alternative scenarios.

Given the hard, black seed of intention.
Given the lack of funereal platitudes,
implicit silence. Given *pulse, no pulse.*
Given Jack with his fistful of beans
and no instructions—just his mother's
disdain. Given the broken earpiece
on the secret telephone. Given the echoing
hurt, back-up singers disappearing behind
you into silent shadow while you're shouting
into the mike *get me out of this bad dream—*

miracle canceled due to weak sales, fire
in the box office. Given the lack of generic
substitutes and the overabundance of slurs.
Given mad calculations—how many, how far,
how fast, uninterrupted un-woken and—
say it—unloved, based on lack of tremors
in the delivery of water. The wait, and in the wait,
the length of time greater than wingless flight,
bombastic bullets, the bleeding, the sudden snag
of rope. How much sharpening does a guillotine

need? How much honing based on the scale
weighing betrayal with the heavy thumb
of rejection? Given the forethought and after-
thought regarding final notes. Given how long
to fill in ovals on the final. Given brutal erasers,
tearing paper. I could be wrong about timing,
given my track record of losses. Given
the proximity of falling bodies to my own—
shared rooms, apartments, houses—why did I
not catch a whiff? Given bad connections,
static, given *lost in the mail* and *return*
to sender. Given the time bomb of my own
mad clock. Given the old math, of *carry the one.*
Given stopping the count out of mercy
or self-interest, or throwing in the towel,
the judges' scorecards melting in the immediate
heat, the ring filled with flung debris,
the grieving crowd's furious booing,
someone shouting that the fix was in.
We, the living, pick up the chant.

The Yellow Cave

Leaves on trees bordering
  the trail glow yellow
bright brilliant tunnel
  before falling.
You should know
  the name of those trees
that light your path
  two weeks each year.

De*press*ion. Inadequate name
  watery dish soap
cheap hair dye
  that flopped on the market.
Slow leak of joy patched,
  re-patched, glue dissolving
into unexplained grief, patch bubbling up
  peeling off the hiss of *press*.

  Cave or tunnel?
Tunnel suggests exit.
  Cave, dead-end darkness.
The inadequacy of the name, the lack
  of healing. The flimsy
backdrop of a cheap Western
  collapsing in the desert.
Yellow canopy
  hyped-up heaven

light through leaves
  but not light itself.
Not life itself, but
  a cold path—
blown-down leaves
  slick with wetness.
If you could touch
  the leaves, not just

admire them before they fall.
  If only they came
when you called
  and you could slide
them on like sleeves,
  a suit to greet
the coming snow. *If*
  only/if/only/if/—

a bird cries, hidden in those trees,
  a bird that didn't fly south
stuck here like you
  to wait it out.

Hitting the Bullseye of Depression

Having been here before,
I recognize the landmarks

as I pay for parking
and begin the long hike

from the potholed parking lot,
ignoring the shuttle bus

on principle or desperation,
exaggerating my limp.

I am only just beginning
to enter the sadness arcade

pushing my way through
the barred one-way gate

but I already have the lack
of rules memorized. All I know

is that I'm tall enough
to go on all the rides.

MegaEverything

Nevertheless

If it's a contest to see who has the worst
life, none of us with computers

or pianos will win. We line up to tell
our versions—poignant, heroic tales

of woe—hoping someone licks
a gold star, sticks it to our forehead.

Did you eat all of your vegetables?
I ate all of my vegetables. Even

canned peas, even mushy asparagus.
None of us with vegetables would win.

My cousin's ex-husband's grandmother
once met a starving child in Africa.

If the choice is kill yourself
or write a poem. If you kill yourself

to write a poem. If you write a poem
about killing yourself but do not

kill yourself. Then—then—don't kill
yourself, okay? Play a game

on your computer. Cheat so you win.
Count your lucky stars. Me,

I've got a box full of them
ready to be licked, the box

as light as a feather. The feather
that floats above all our grasping.

MegaEverything

Generals gathered in their masses,
just like witches at black masses.
Evil minds that plot destruction,
sorcerer of death's construction.
—"War Pigs," Black Sabbath

The kid with stringy, blond hair
and torn Megadeth T-shirt
plagiarized song lyrics in his poem.
Black Sabbath? I said.
In my tiny office, he idly kicked
the metal desk, not meeting
my eyes. But then, he never did.

*

1972. Michigan State Fairgrounds.
Black Sabbath ripped through the sharp
muffle of "Paranoid" on the distant stage
while I guzzled malt liquor from quart bottles
on a gloomy Saturday afternoon.

Ozzy stalking onstage scared me
in a familiar Detroit way—like a biker gang
crashing a high school party—I shook
it off. I raised my fist.

*

He said turning in the lyrics was a test
but would go no further. Had I passed?
Those lyrics, the only semi-coherent thing
he'd turned in all term.

He could've fooled me with Megadeth lyrics.
Perhaps he had. We agreed that he should
drop the class. He hesitated at the door
like there might be one more thing.

*

Sixteen. My ears buzzed
with dark-star feedback—
barking dogs, bloody teeth, fragments
of a thorough ass-kicking.

Ozzy's wire-cutter voice asked
what happened when we died
and where exactly was the soul?
When a thunderstorm arced down on us,
no one fled. We stood and took it.

*

Poetry was all I had that wasn't toxic.
I should've been easier on the kid.
His name was Chris. He slumped away,
black boots clomping against the floor,
and I never saw him again.

*

The bitter mascara of the unrepentant
and the flawed jewel of self-absorption.
Ozzy hadn't yet bitten the head
off a bat when I saw him in '72.

He only had to do it once. The rest of us,
Chris, we think about it every day
under the black incoherent moon.

Lifetime High

The heaviest thing I ever stole?
A twelve-pound bowling ball. Strangest thing
I ever found on my lawn? A bowling ball
I did not steal—swirly green, drilled
for tinier fingers. I took it to my office
and rolled it across the floor, regaling
colleagues with the mystery of its arrival.
Regaled! In the era of bowling shirt chic,
bowling shoes chic, I one-upped them all.

I loved its solid thundering thud
when dropped on tile. One day, I rolled it
all the way down the long, sloped hallway,
and while I can easily find my university's
ranking (23rd), I cannot find the length of what
is said to be Pittsburgh's longest continuous hallway.

How can I determine how far my ball traversed
before clonking off the wall? Has any
bowling ball ever *traversed* before? I did not
hear it clonk, having run screaming
from the building that Sunday afternoon.

I walked out of Bronco Lanes back in Detroit
that Friday night—I could drink a lot and still
not stagger, a skinny guy who could hold his liquor,
and, looking back from the dry state of Sobervania,
I wish he couldn't. If you look for me back in
the seventies and eighties and a rotten rind
of the nineties, you'll find me at the table
drinking everyone else under it.
Why? In that numb sloshy splash zone,
that question was not entertained
nor amused. That question was sent out
into the dark somber non-party night.

Last year, I bowled a 189—lifetime high!—
at my nephew Philip's birthday. Hilarity
did not ensue. Defeated, he wept into
the hand dryer and disgorged his hot dog.

I stuck my fingers in a twelve-pounder—I threw
a light ball. I drank a heavy ball. I danced
my bowling alley slip-and-slide out through
Bronco's door and cracked-tar parking lot
and through the gravel parking lot
of Arco Tool & Die where night shift
stood outside on break smoking, guffawing
as I lugged my house ball with the give-away stripe
past them, briefly sober and sad.

I own the bowling shirt of Big Jack Saworski
who died in his fifties, despite his perfect
mowed head of hair—asbestos lodged in his lungs.
My parents bowled in a mixed-doubles league
with him and Milly—Milly who takes my blind mother
out once a month now, though others abandoned
her to books-on-tape and her talking watch,
tilted back in the living room La-Z-Boy.

Oh, I am about to weep into the hand dryer,
Philip. Philip, it's no big deal—did I tell you
the one about stealing the bowling ball?
Did I tell you about the swirly green one
that showed up on my lawn?

In the middle of Otis Street, I did my approach-
and-release, though I could not glide on concrete.
The ball clunked down the pocked street till it rolled
into Eight Mile Road, the main drag of Detroit's border,
on its long unmeasured journey—guffaw guffaw—

to end up on my front lawn 300 miles
and years away in Pittsburgh.

I wish it was the stupidest thing I ever did.
Nobody got killed, but cars were inconvenienced.
Maybe somebody even joked, *hey, a bowling ball*
broke through the Bronco corral! Guffaw.

I had a lot more stupid to do before I ended up
in Sobervania, bowling down the longest hallway
in the world on a Sunday afternoon in a vacant
university building in the bowling shirt
of the late Big Jack Saworski, passing
that ball on to someone somewhere
who might need it more.

The Crucial Lack of Redemption

I quit drinking when it turned into a part-time job.
—Ted Kooser

I studied Spanish for years and years
but never learned to roll my R's. Like an engine
not turning over, slowly wearing the battery
down. This, after it took me eight years
of remedial speech to correct the slurring
of my words. This, before I began to drink
myself into slurring again. Though even
drunk I could not roll, could not flutter
those beautiful syllables. My father
never learned to say I love you
or use a computer or GPS. I've wasted
great quantities of unspare change
considering what is willful and what
cannot be helped and what
cannot be blamed. Lift the hood
and peer under as if something
could be done. Sometimes you just
have to slam it back down
and walk away. I'm a pretty good
walker, I've learned, wearing out
shoes and blues on city sidewalks
rubbing shoulders against brick for luck.
If I tell you I stopped drinking, that might
suggest a certain redemption, but there's
always that matter of the R's circling
like flocks of black birds in December
that I can never name.

Catholic

Your own personal Jesus
Someone to hear your prayers
Someone who cares
—Martin Gore

In my cold toes, I feel where Jesus left and never came back. I often eat fish on Fridays, so maybe there's some remnant in my gut. At 65, I feel a slight unsteadiness growing when I stand, the soul beginning to lift from the body. Catholic school and church—nuns with giant swaggering rosaries, priests with secret mumblings—easy targets, even in dark confessionals. Balloons filled with holy water bursting like Biblical flashes of life. I'm looking for the harder targets of kindness and peace. Friends who never lost the faith—steady flames simmering in their hearts, still moon-walking for Jesus. I admit envy now. If only I could walk my own self backwards into those tiny footprints. But I've pretty much filled them all with cement, even back to first steps. No rocket ship to Planet Jesus. I once tried to explain Easter to my daughter but could not answer her innocent questions about the *ions*—crucifixion, resurrection, nor where to purchase such nails. *Does cruci-fiction mean its fiction?* Fish is good for you. Suffering, not so much. We never got to transubstantiation, one of the longest words I know—I stop believing before I'm even done pronouncing it. I've been reading the list of dead classmates from high school as the thread lengthens. Is it thickening or fraying? Somebody in charge of crimping on new black beads to our holy rosary of the dead. I steady myself against the wall of all my friends who keep the faith, just to put on another pair of socks.

Dinner at Lynn and Linda's with Ken and Jack

Watch the International Space Station pass overhead from several thousand worldwide locations. It is the third brightest object in the sky and easy to spot if you know when to look up.

Dinner tonight with two married gay couples
and their kids. The women have a boy.
The men have a girl. Off playing
video games in the basement.

*

Growing up in Detroit, our imaginations
limited by polluted night sky, oblivious
to constellations of shame, we teased
each other for admiring the moon.
I never looked both ways
before I crossed the street.

*

Linda looks it up on her phone.
Lynn rolls her eyes. Still, we step out
onto the porch at 8:17 in Pittsburgh,
on October 23, and wait. We have not
turned our furnaces on, any of us,
but we will soon. Couples lean
into each other for balance
on this dizzy planet.

*

Linda serves tamarinds. None of us
have tried them before. For dessert,
we eat donuts decorated with dulled
vampire teeth and blurry witches—
who can make anything graceful

on a donut? They're made to be gripped
with certainty and bit into and swallowed.
We discuss donuts and memories
of donuts and Halloween and costumes
we will no longer wear forever.

*

The kids stay inside. No interest
in seeing bright light zipper silent
across the sky, but the rest of us wait,
as we have waited for many things.
Porchlight off, so as not to interfere,
yet tonight, we have found our way home.

*

After it passes, we go back in
to round up kids, deal with life on earth.
The girl asleep in a father's arms,
the boy on the safe couch of dreamland.

*

Outside, we said nothing,
then we said *wow*—even that
too much in the grand silence
of changing seasons. Does the crew
circling the earth ever tire of wonder?

Ken's from Michigan, like me
with the flat vowels. Jack
was my student thirty years ago
and engaged to marry his girlfriend.

Linda, my wife's oldest
and best friend. Linda and Lynn.
The Linns. What made her think
to watch the space station pass?

A white dot moving across the sky,
not a falling star, or a star at all.
I guess the kids take it for granted
what we can do now, the sky seamless,
not falling.

Nightmare of My Last Class Before Retirement

They kicked me out of my classroom
in the middle of my last lecture,
in the middle of a sentence
that began with *I remember*.
They needed the room
for routine ritual bloodletting
or emergency vacuuming.
(something something dream smoke)

I led my students out through
the gauntlet of the disgruntled self-satisfied
whose skin glistened with oily retribution
they'd been saving up for years
like belly button lint and ear wax.
(even the hallway disappeared)

They sent us to the only space available
for finishing up my illustrious career:
the local driving range. I abandoned
my notes, my grade book, my accumulated
wisdom. We all got a bucket of balls.
(such comfort to see the range balls
striped red and blue to prevent theft!)

Everyone got into it, hacking and whacking
until finding beyond all reason a sweet spot
to send one flying. I myself had trouble
getting air under the ball—lots of line drives
that bounced then rolled.
(two states away, near the horse track
by the old factory where I once toiled)

Of course, we all tried to aim our shots
to hit the caged tractor retrieving balls
out on the range. I must brag that I was the one
who finally nailed it. Oh, loud clanging ricochet!
()

I discovered that I was the one driving the tractor—
both shooter and victim—and woke up.
(against my will)

I took this as an omen never to take up
golfing on actual courses, to rely on
the range's defined limits. I suddenly
remembered leaving all my notes
in that stuffy classroom and imagined
the harumphers (authorities suggest this word
has a second r, but it doesn't look right to me)

scouring them for evidence of my unfitness
(though they didn't need it!)
It might have been nice to watch the notes
blow away across that stretch of green.
Perhaps that tractor I was driving
could've shredded them as they surged
past the rusty 200-yard marker.
Driving ranges are like bowling alleys!
(This great insight carries me
into retirement and beyond.)

I was using the ancient clubs I'd found
in my grandfather's basement after he died.
My grandfather, who putted around
cigarette butts on the par 3 course
on Belle Isle in Detroit and always came
home with more balls than he'd started with.
(This all wasn't in the dream. If you can't
take liberties with a dream, well . . .)

My grandfather tried to teach me a few things.
Never say *Fore!* he said.
Keep your head down, he said.

Final Miracle Before Retiring from Slowpitch

My latest prayer consists of nonsense syllables
based on the friction of two sticks rubbing together.
The best kind of nonsense, I've decided, no clever-
ness about it. I prefer people to pat me on the ass

rather than stab me in the back, but I've obtained
good drugs for stab wounds. I can't pronounce
them, but they all contain the prefix or suffix *damn.*
Until recently, I still played softball

and occasionally got a pat on the ass.
Then, at age 60, I got taken out at second base
by a young man with a limited vocabulary.
Rubbing two sticks together requires a certain

patience. And perhaps at least a slight belief
in some higher power. If the guy had just asked,
I'd have said, Sure, you can be safe, dude,
just don't go breaking that rib God took

from Adam and gave to me. Lying
in dirt, trying to catch my breath,
which had a mind of its own, staggering away
into an overcast sky, I could only gasp out

my nonsense. On my hands and knees—
the position for prayer I've finally landed on.
Was my foot on the bag?
Did I hold onto the ball long enough?

I rubbed two ribs together
and burst into flame.

The Lunar Module Stage of Life

starts around fifty
  and ends when you die
it involves lightheaded claustrophobia
  and memory-loss mattresses

a lack of home cooking
  and the betrayal of ancient color photos
it starts when you lose your glasses
  and ends with political tunnel vision

it involves long goodbyes
  then short goodbyes
dreams of melted crayons
  and the smell of Play-Doh

an emphasis on plumbing
  not birth control
it involves a new twist on fate
  and a return to sacraments

sincere wishing at wishing wells
  and comparing notes on backs, knees,
and the parts that used to be naughty,
  but still failing the eye test, any test

it involves hair or lack thereof,
  pill counting and more pillows,
sleep or the lack thereof
  and hiring a house painter

jiggling the handle
  and lowering your standards
estimating your pre-adolescent
  and post-retirement income

imaginary demolition derbies
  and fender gender benders
it involves random blame
  and inspirational messages

fewer photographs
  more peeing
it involves the whitewashing
  of sex and the black funeral suit

obituaries not comics
  lists not paragraphs
the opposite of zero gravity
  and caving in on yourself

it involves defying
  in lieu of stiffening
faith in splashdown
  in lieu of drowning

it involves staring at the moon
  and the moon staring back
and the silent light
  and the light silence.

The Secret Agent Briefcase

When I got my professor gig, my parents
bought me a hard-sided briefcase
with a combination lock. You could sit on it.

Stand in principle on it. Smack it upside your
head to get your smarts going. You could not
squeeze many books into it. When I pressed

the latches and it clicked open, I expected
to see a bomb. I carried it to school
my first fall until a colleague joked

You got a bomb in there? He called me
The Secret Agent, though I stopped using it
immediately. It sat in my bedroom closet

with slippers I never wore. Thanks,
Mom and Dad. I gave it to Goodwill last week
with a load of my children's outgrown clothes.

Some guy down on his luck is going to love
that briefcase—to mess with his friends,
to absorb strange looks from downtowners

passing his homeless station. Perhaps he will
fill it with meaningful papers or half-eaten
sandwiches or the holy relics of his tough life.

When I got my gig, two years removed
from the line at Ford's beside my father,
I had a couple bad habits and a trunk full

of good luck, driving from Detroit to Pittsburgh
with enough drugs to last till I found a local dealer.
A new pair of shoes blistered my feet.

The drugs nearly covered the shame
of my blunt speech in that nuanced landscape
of betrayal. No wonder, blisters. No wonder,

the bomb. I used the briefcase years later
as a prop for a movie I made that no one saw,
making it that much more experimental

and noteworthy in my annual report. I carry
my books in a backpack and my shame
in a secret pocket. I have less of it

these days—the old professor, survivor
of fake bomb threats in petty emails.
I was a secret agent after all.

A double agent. An agent who carved
his own decoder ring at weekly meetings
of the special club where the man

with my briefcase might appear
someday, just when I need him.
My parents came to town

when I got my endowed chair.
My blind mother in her green raincoat.
My father in his funeral overcoat.

I myself purchased a suit.
The hors d'oeuvres were tasteless,
but my father enjoyed the novelty

of stuffed mushrooms, and my mother,
the mini eggrolls. I circled them like a dog
protecting its wounded master.

Though who was wounded?
I keep my old factory lunch bucket
in my office at the university,

dull gray scratches, dents
in black paint. I rub it for luck
before meetings of the committee

on screechy chairs. If that seems
like sad nostalgia to you,
perhaps you're right.

But it too is hard.
It too protects what's inside.

Living Without a Horse

I don't know how I've done it
for 66 years. I once found
a rusted horseshoe walking
through a muddy field
one spring day in mid-Michigan
and hung it upside down
like you're supposed to.

And I did throw them clanging
against stakes in the traditional game.
And I did get shocked
by an electric fence
trying to pet a horse once.
And I did bet on which
was the fastest two or three
boozy evenings on the rail.

And I did try to ride one once
on a family outing
though I missed
having a steering wheel
and held the reins
like a dog clenching its own
leash between its teeth.

And my older brother argued
with the farmer when the ride
lasted only 45 minutes
not the hour we paid for.

That argument shames me now.
We were from Detroit
and used to the precision of cars,
the strict keeping track
of gauges and meters.

Horses—such stunning creatures
shaking their manes in the sun.
And telling jokes I'll never understand.
And running with the grace
of wind-blown grass.

The horseshoe did not bring me luck.
And I left it above the door
of that old brown house
in mid-Michigan
after one lover left
and another died suddenly—
the one who'd help me
find it in that wet field
springing into green.

I've left a lot of things behind
in my years here.
And buried a lot of friends.
And looked at a lot of horses
looking at me
over electric fences.

Fifteen more minutes on a horse
wouldn't have made any difference.
But on cold, wet spring days,
wind blowing into my face,
maybe lifting my long hair up
into the air just a bit,
I like to imagine it would.

At 65

This morning I fell back
  into deep snow
and dug myself into a snow angel.

Yeah. I didn't tell anyone. I mean,
  c'mon, right?
Who did I think I was kidding?

I woke up then, as if touched
  by, not God, or iced fever,
but—some lost tender spirit?

What I want to say is that
  when I stood, I suddenly
lost all grace and nearly

fell onto my angel. My hand-
  print to save myself
lies where my heart is/was/

should be, a badge of snow
  in the dusted grass.
I noticed then the size

of my wings, their broad
  graceful arc—
who made those? I asked

as snow continued falling.
  I looked up into it,
almost dazzled again

  at 65.

Tunnel to Canada

The Detroit–Windsor tunnel connects the cities of Detroit, Michigan, and Windsor, Ontario, Canada. It is the second-busiest crossing between the United States and Canada, the first being the Ambassador Bridge, which also connects the two cities, which are situated on the Detroit River.

"I seem to recall a dumbass teen that stuck his head out of the car in the Windsor/Detroit tunnel and got decapitated on a pillar."

I looked forward to crossing the Ambassador Bridge
but ended up in the Tunnel to Canada
that has no grand name or view.

An old girlfriend from out of state
thought Tunnel to Canada was the name
of a downtown restaurant.

I emerged into the light to answer questions
at the border after accidentally drifting
into the frequent-flyer lane.

My life has been a series of gentle decapitations
and yet another curious head pops up again
in suspicious wonder at survival.

Out of the darkness into the light
and already angry men asking questions
about changing lanes. *Oh, Canada,*
I hum in my own anxious tunnel.

They have been so nice to me in Canada
I want to end every sentence I write with Canada.

I have burned many inelegant bridges.
Nothing like the bridges
to Canada. I want to end every sentence with bridges.

I misspelled inelegant so that it looks like intelligent.
I have also burned many intelligent
bridges with my Stupidity Matches—
waterproof, strike anywhere matches.

I want to end every sentence with matches.
Don't play with matches.
I never lit a tennis match.
I never played a match

made in heaven.
I want to end every sentence with heaven.

I had a good meal at Tunnel to Canada.
It's a nude restaurant, but the novelty
has worn off. Clothes are back.
The lights are back
on. It's turning into a dark restaurant.

The meal was all potato chips
and poker chips.
A special at the casino.

It is hard to end many lines with casino
given that Windsor only has one.
Finally, Detroit legalized casinos
to compete with Windsor's casino.

Though for many years I was a dumbass
teen, I was never beheaded and continued as a dumbass
in my twenties.

They finally let me go through customs
at the end of the tunnel, without even searching
me. Me, I am still searching.

Dusk

Okay, it's quiet here now, and we can talk. Here and now being relative things. A cracked cement slab of a porch, the blur between day and night. Quiet being a relative thing, given the chattering cicadas in the trees I can't see. Just leaves, barely swaying in light breeze, like I'm in some lazy nightclub after hours, the only one left, nowhere to go, or perhaps it's the one place I want to be. The light, muted orange, the smell, muted orange. Good light for dancing alone to percussion. Or a lack of percussion, even our own hearts smoothening into graceful, subtle waves without spikes or plunges. I said we can talk, which means we don't have to. We have to breathe, to not think about breathing. The imperative shrugs its head and closes its eyes. Hovering solitude. I'm swimming toward, not away, water barely stirring through my cupped hands.